GALATIANS

GALATIANS

Life in the New Creation

A SPIRITUAL-PASTORAL READING

RONALD D. WITHERUP

Paulist Press
New York / Mahwah, NJ

Cover image by Philip Meyer / Shutterstock.com
Cover design by Sharyn Banks
Book design by Lynn Else

Library of Congress Cataloging-in-Publication Data
Names: Witherup, Ronald D., 1950– author.
Title: Galatians : life in the new creation-a spiritual-pastoral reading / Ronald D Witherup.
Description: New York : Paulist Press, 2020. | Includes bibliographical references and index.
Identifiers: LCCN 2018056140 (print) | LCCN 2019000781 (ebook) | ISBN 9780809154036 (pbk. : alk. paper)
Subjects: LCSH: Bible. Galatians—Commentaries. | Christian life—Catholic authors.
Classification: LCC BS2685.53 .W58 2020 (print) | LCC BS2685.53 (ebook) | DDC 227/.4077—dc23
LC record available at https://lccn.loc.gov/2018056140
LC ebook record available at https://lccn.loc.gov/2019000781

ISBN 978-0-8091-5403-6 (paperback)
ISBN 978-1-58768-781-5 (e-book)

Published by Paulist Press
997 Macarthur Boulevard
Mahwah, New Jersey 07430
www.paulistpress.com

Printed and bound in the
United States of America

In memory of Augustin Cardinal Bea and the
Fathers of Vatican Council II (1962–65),
whose faithful scholarship and selfless dedication to the
word of God led to the promulgation of *Dei Verbum*,
the Dogmatic Constitution on Divine Revelation
November 18, 1965,
which, in turn, fostered a rediscovery of
the Bible among Catholics

CONTENTS

LIST OF ILLUSTRATIONS

LIST OF MAPS AND TABLES

MAPS

TABLES

PREFACE

After many fits and starts, this "reading" of Galatians has finally come to fruition. I feel somewhat like a character in "A Funny Thing Happened on the Way to…" plot because nothing quite turned out how I intended it. This project began as a totally different commentary, but numerous factors, including an unexpected surgery, intervened to prevent that from becoming a reality. Even the dedication hints at the delay. I had intended for this book to appear around the time of the fiftieth anniversary of Vatican Council II (1962–65), which was the single most important event in the Catholic Church in the twentieth century, and which fostered the modern Catholic approach to the Bible that is now commonplace. My own interests in biblical studies have dovetailed considerably with Vatican II, as I have devoted some of my research to questions about a Catholic approach to the Bible and the impact of *Dei Verbum*, the Council's Dogmatic Constitution on Divine Revelation. I have retained the dedication because it is still worthy, as explained below.

Another impetus for this book comes from having taught the letters of Paul for many years, either in the classroom or through many conferences, congresses, and symposiums. The Letter to the Galatians attracted me because it is a fiery letter, filled with passion, but it is also not always easy to understand. James D. G. Dunn, one of the premier recent commentators on Paul, summarizes it well: "In no sense is Galatians an ivory tower tract remote from real life, the dispassionate statement of one high above the battle. Rather, it is a cry from the heart of one at the very front of the line of Christian advance, dealing with questions which determined the identity and whole life-style of those to whom he wrote" (Dunn, *Theology*, 1). Essentially, many commentaries get mired in the intricacies of the theological argumentation of the letter and tend to miss the impact of other aspects that might be less self-evident but are nonetheless present. So, I felt the urge to provide a spiritual-pastoral *reading* of Galatians primarily for educated laypeople, priests, deacons, pastors, catechists, seminarians, or any interested readers of the Bible whose familiarity with Paul's letters sometimes founders on the difficulties of understanding the Apostle's writings. This is a commentary that would at the same time provoke thought, but not be so demanding as to discourage the average reader from engaging such an interesting letter. Paul's letters are, admittedly, not easy to comprehend. It is worth recalling the words of Second Peter, whose judgment of Paul's letters has a ring of truth even today: "In them there are some things hard to comprehend, which the ignorant and unstable twist to their own destruction, just as they do the other scriptures" (2 Pet 3:16b). So we are in good company if we admit occasionally our inability to understand Paul's letters. And because of the intended audience, I do not engage in detailing too many complicated scholarly disputes, except where it seems essential. Rather, I hope that my reading of Galatians is coherent and simple enough to provide interested readers with a solid overview of the letter and its importance.

Other reasons present themselves for choosing Galatians. First, although thematically related to Paul's formidable Letter to the Romans, Galatians is one of Paul's most personal letters. Paul's autobiography forms an important backdrop to the letter. Galatians allows us to glimpse Paul the person amid heated apologetic argument and emotional pique regarding one of his dear communities that he felt was in danger of abandoning their hard-won faith. Second, Galatians is a much shorter and less systematic letter than Romans, which limits the number of themes that need to be considered and keeps our focus on how Paul's theology shaped his pastoral relationships and, vice versa, how his relationships had an impact on the shape of his theological reflection. In fact, this bidirectional movement is one of my specific interests in reading Galatians as a faith-filled Christian. A third reason concerns the letter's extensive teaching on freedom, a theme that is especially attractive to Americans. While some consider Romans *the* letter on Christian freedom, Galatians is far more direct on this theme, especially as it relates to the nature of "life in the new creation." Fourth, the letter has also had an enormous influence on the great Protestant-Catholic divide since the time of the Protestant Reformation. It is fortuitous, perhaps, that this book is being published soon after the year that Protestants celebrated the five hundredth anniversary of the Reformation, usually dated from the occasion when Martin Luther posted his ninety-five theses and altered Christian history (October 31, 1517). In fact, Luther, despite having come to the realization of the importance of "justification by faith" from reading the Letter to the Romans, considered Galatians *his* letter. He famously wrote, "The Epistle to the Galatians is my epistle; I have betrothed myself to it; it is my Katherine, my wife." While I have mixed feelings about placing too much emphasis on such a traumatic event as the Reformation, which divided the Body of Christ, I am nevertheless convinced of the importance of bringing Catholic and Protestant interpretations of Paul's letters into alignment, while respecting differences that are bound to persist.

Indeed, this commentary is neither distinctively nor overtly Catholic, although inevitably I approach it from my own Catholic background. I have made a concerted effort to draw into the commentary, wherever appropriate, pertinent insights from the Catholic tradition, while remaining open to the larger living Christian tradition of the faith from the beginning of Christianity. Having done my doctoral studies at a Presbyterian seminary, where at the time I was the token Roman Catholic in the student body, I learned an enormous amount from my Protestant professors and fellow students. They helped to broaden my own approach to biblical studies in ways I could scarcely have imagined. In this book on Galatians, I will try to bring that to bear on my reading of the letter, without pretending to surmount totally my own Catholic approach or the inevitable differences between Protestant and Catholic interpretation. I believe these interpretations should be mutually enriching and should not contribute to the divide that persists. Furthermore, as will become apparent in the commentary, there are new, compelling reasons to applaud a common approach to Paul's letters, especially Galatians, because of ecumenical dialogues that happily began after Vatican II and have borne much fruit.

Some of the distinctive elements of this commentary are the sidebars: the "Living Christian Tradition of the Church" (which note passages from the history of interpretation or other materials from church tradition); the "Biblical Background" (which explain in more detail certain concepts from Scripture or parallel passages); the "Cultural and Historical Background" (information that fleshes out life in Paul's day); the sections offering "Pastoral and Spiritual Reflection;" and the "Questions for Discussion," which are useful for individuals seeking to reflect more deeply on Galatians, or for group study of the letter. Note, however, there is not a pastoral or spiritual comment for every passage of Galatians, since it is not always possible to have a one-to-one correspondence for pastoral or spiritual application from a modern perspective. Nonetheless, the comments that are included will be helpful. In three of the appendices, there are a substantial number of comments from a Catholic perspective—liturgy, the *Catechism of the Catholic Church*, and Vatican Council II—because many Catholics may not be aware of how influential Paul's letters have really been in Catholic tradition. However, as noted, I have tried to be ecumenical in my reading, drawing on the insights from many authors who have interpreted the letter from within a Protestant framework. The commentaries of Martin Luther and John Calvin, for instance, remain very valuable, provided one can overlook some of the severely anti-Catholic sentiment contained in them. My approach, therefore, is in line with the ecumenical perspective that was a hallmark of the Second Vatican Council.

Because of the intended audience, I have composed a "one-stop shopping" approach to Galatians for those who do not have much experience with commentaries or who perhaps don't have the time or inclination to pursue background issues. Thus, with the aid of charts, tables, maps, sidebars, and images, both the history of interpretation of this letter and its multiple contributions to the Christian tradition support my reading and explanation of the letter. Additionally, the book comes with access to more materials on the internet that contain further information in downloadable formats that might be especially useful to students, professors, or Bible study groups. Visit "Online Resources" at www.paulistpress.com. I have endeavored to keep footnotes and explanations of Greek words to a minimum, without passing over essentials, and I do not pursue detailed discussions with the opinions of other scholars, except where I think important material might be of interest to this broader audience. I have, however, benefited enormously from their scholarship, and have noted in the bibliography those commentaries or books that I have consulted the most. I have adopted the shorthand method of referring to these resources, when necessary, using only the name and page number within parentheses, such as (Matera, 25), unless further information is needed for clarity. For an exhaustive bibliography, readers could consult one of the larger commentaries on Galatians, such as that of J. Louis Martyn. I have only noted resources that I have used or that can be recommended for the intended audience.

Regarding the translation, although the NRSV is cited for many biblical texts, I have chosen to use my own translation of Galatians throughout. It is found as a unified text in appendix I, though I cite it passage by passage within the commentary. In fact, my comments are on sections of the letter, not line by line. My goal has been to capture Paul's message by "sense packages," as he advances his arguments throughout the letter. Reading the entire letter at one sitting provides a good orientation and is a good exercise in getting the sweep of Paul's argumentation. I have tried to keep the translation as literal as possible to preserve both the "flavor" and, at times, the ambiguity of the text, yet to render it in understandable contemporary English. Every translation is an interpretation, and I have used the main English versions as a way of comparing my understanding with these more familiar editions.

The dedication indicates my orientation. In desiring to pay homage to *Dei Verbum* on its golden anniversary, I honor the multitude of bishops and scholars who were behind the drafting of this highly influential document, one of the most important to come from the ecumenical Council. *Dei Verbum* specifically called for ecumenical translations and study editions of the Bible that could profitably be used by *"all Christians"* (*DV* 25). In addition, its nuanced teaching on Sacred Scripture and Tradition in the Catholic Church gave further impetus for Catholic scholars to continue their research under the guidance of the magisterium of the church, while also promoting better appreciation of the Sacred Scriptures among all the people of God (*DV* 26). Thus, *Dei Verbum* encouraged Catholic participation in ecumenical translations and interpretation, which is why I do not limit myself only to Catholic resources. I single out the name of the German Jesuit Augustin Cardinal Bea (1881–1968), among the many who profitably contributed to the final text of *Dei Verbum*, because of his specific leadership in drafting the document. Bea, who served as president of the Holy See's Secretariat for Christian Unity (1960–68) and thereby contributed greatly to ecumenical and interfaith discussions during the Council, was himself a biblical scholar. On scriptural matters and the preparation of *Dei Verbum*, he was instrumental in assuring that the results of modern biblical scholarship did not fall by the wayside during the long debates from 1962 to 1965, when the fate of the constitution on revelation awaited resolution of seemingly endless discussions and compromises to arrive at an acceptable final draft.[1] The entire church owes him a debt of gratitude.

ACKNOWLEDGMENTS

Paulist Press has been most generous in accepting this spiritual-pastoral commentary on Galatians, which is a considerably expanded version of my small commentary on the same letter published in *The Paulist Biblical Commentary* (2018). I thank Father Mark-David Janus, CSP, the publisher, for his initial openness to this project. I also express sincere gratitude for the team at Paulist Press, who has been instrumental in various aspects of preparing and promoting the manuscript.

Although I alone am responsible for whatever failings this brief commentary may contain, I am grateful to several people with whom conversations helped clarify my own thoughts about Galatians and Paul's theology. In particular, the participants of the Catholic Biblical Association's Task Force on "God in the Letters of Paul," which has been meeting annually for some years, assisted my thought processes by posing key observations and questions that gave me much food for thought. Also, I thank my friend and colleague Father Frank J. Matera, formerly of the Catholic University of America and now pastor of St. Mary's Parish in Simsbury, Connecticut, for his own expert commentary on Galatians (not to mention his fine book on Pauline theology, listed in the bibliography) and his helpful encouragement along the circuitous route of this manuscript. I am also grateful to Father Thomas Stegman, SJ, dean and *Professor Ordinarius* of the Boston College School of Theology and Ministry, for his patient encouragement and his careful editing of a shorter version of this commentary. My confrere, Father Thomas R. Hurst, PSS, former president rector of St. Mary's Seminary and University in Baltimore, Maryland, where he still serves as an adjunct professor in patristics and Bible, rendered great service by his careful reading of the text and offering numerous suggestions to ensure accuracy, consistency, and comprehensibility. In addition, the librarian, Thomas Raszewski, and the entire library staff of St. Mary's Seminary and University have always been most gracious in accommodating my requests for assistance and materials; for their many kindnesses, I am most grateful.

As I conclude this project, I feel compelled to adopt as my own the honest sentiment of the author of 2 Maccabees: "If the result is well told and to the point, that is what I myself intended; if it is poorly done and mediocre, that is the best I could do" (2 Macc 15:38).

R. D. W.
Paris, September 14, 2019
Feast of the Exaltation of the Holy Cross

ABBREVIATIONS

AB	Anchor Bible
ABRL	Anchor Bible Reference Library
ACCS	Ancient Christian Commentary on Scripture
ANTC	Abingdon New Testament Commentaries
au. trans.	author's translation
AYBRL	Anchor Yale Bible Reference Library
BBC	Blackwell Bible Commentaries
BNTC	Black's New Testament Commentaries
CaE	*Cahiers évangile*
CBNT	Commentaires bibliques: Nouveau Testament
CCC	*Catechism of the Catholic Church* (2nd ed., 1998)
CGPEP	Theodore of Mopsuestia. *Catena Graecorum partum in espistulas Pauli*. Edited by J. A. Cramer. Oxford: Clarendon, 1842–1854
ConC	Concordia Commentary
Gk.	Greek
Heb.	Hebrew
JANT	*The Jewish Annotated New Testament*. 2nd ed. Edited by Amy-Jill Levine and Marc Zvi Brettler. New York: Oxford University Press, 2017
Lat.	Latin
lit.	literally
LD	Lectio Divina
LNTS	Library of New Testament Studies
LXX	The Septuagint (Greek translation of the OT)
NABRE	The New American Bible, Revised Edition (2011)
NAS	New American Standard Bible (1995)

NEB	New English Bible
NET	New English Translation (NET Bible; a free electronic edition of the Bible available on the Internet at https://net.bible.org)
NIB	*The New Interpreter's Bible*. Edited by Leander E. Keck, et al. 12 vols. Nashville: Abingdon, 1994–2004
NIGTC	New International Greek Testament Commentary
NIV	New International Version
NJB	New Jerusalem Bible
NJBC	*New Jerome Biblical Commentary*. Edited by Raymond E. Brown et al. Englewood Cliffs, NJ: Prentice-Hall, 1990
NRSV	New Revised Standard Version
NT	New Testament
NTE	The New Testament for Everyone
NTL	New Testament Library
OECS	Oxford Early Christian Studies
OT	Old Testament
PDV	*Pastores Dabo Vobis*, Postsynodal Apostolic Exhortation of Pope John Paul II (1992) on the Formation of Priests
PG	Patrologia Graeca. Edited by J-P. Migne. 166 vols. Paris: Migne, 1857–1886
PL	Patrologia Latina. Edited by J-P. Migne. 221 vols. Paris: Migne, 1844–1864
PO	*Presbyterorum Ordinis*, Vatican Council II's Decree on the Ministry and Life of Priests (1965)
REB	Revised English Bible (1989)
RSV	Revised Standard Version (2nd ed., 1971)
SHBC	Smyth & Helwys Bible Commentary
SP	Sacra Pagina
VD	*Verbum Domini*, Postsynodal Apostolic Exhortation of Pope Benedict XVI (2010) on the Word of God in the Life of the Church
WBC	Word Biblical Commentary

INTRODUCTION

AUTHORSHIP, DATE, PROVENANCE, AND AUDIENCE

All scholars recognize the Letter to the Galatians as one of the seven undisputed letters of Paul, along with Romans, 1—2 Corinthians, Philippians, 1 Thessalonians, and Philemon. More problematic is determining the precise date it was written, its provenance, and the audience it originally addressed. These complex, interrelated issues are not easily resolved with certainty.

Pauline and Deutero-Pauline Letters

Since the advent of modern biblical scholarship in the late eighteenth century, scholars have raised questions about the authorship of many books of the NT. Within the Pauline corpus of thirteen letters, all of which bear his name, all scholars accept seven as being without doubt from Saint Paul. These are Romans, 1 and 2 Corinthians, Galatians, Philippians, 1 Thessalonians, and Philemon.

Six of the letters, however, fall into a category of disputed authorship. They are Ephesians, Colossians, 2 Thessalonians, and the three Pastoral Letters: 1–2 Timothy and Titus. These six are called "Deutero-Pauline," from the Greek expression meaning "second" (*deuter-* or *deutero*), because some scholars believe they were written by disciples of Paul, who were writing in his name at some later date. This practice of attributing authorship to an authoritative person is well attested in the ancient world. The basis for scholars making such decisions on authorship is normally vocabulary, style, and theological perspective.

One could legitimately ask if this distinction really makes a difference. On one level, it does. For example, when a serious difference of conception arises, such as the notion of the church as the Body of Christ, as compared to a more institutional structure seen in the Pastoral Letters, one could say that it represents an important development in theological perspective beyond what Paul himself

1

taught, such as in 1 Corinthians. Or regarding the restriction of women's roles in the church, some believe such passages in Paul's letters reflect a later time when cultural customs were becoming more restrictive; these perspectives do not match Paul's more open approach reflected in the number of his women coworkers (e.g., Rom 16:1-7). From another perspective, however, one could say that the distinction is not that important because all the letters bear Paul's name and are found in the NT. They all constitute the "Pauline tradition"; they are all canonical, inspired Scripture whose spiritual message remains for all time. There are pros and cons to both positions. Also, we must admit that there is no scholarly unanimity regarding Deutero-Pauline authorship for the six disputed letters as scholars offer varying assessments either for or against genuine Pauline authorship.

Fortunately, regarding Galatians, no serious scholar doubts Paul's authorship. We can be confident that the perspective of this letter represents his thoughts insofar as we can interpret them in the context of the letter.

The letter speaks of the "churches of Galatia" (1:1) as the intended recipients. But exactly where is Galatia? As can be seen on the map, two possibilities existed in Paul's day: one was the Galatia of the north, the ethnic region in Asia Minor, modern-day central Turkey; the other possibility was the Roman province of Galatia, which was more to the south.

Asia Minor in the early first century CE

The Acts of the Apostles, which recounts Paul's missionary journeys, does not entirely resolve the issue. On the one hand, Paul is said to have visited and evangelized cities in the southern territory, such as Derbe, Lystra, and Iconium, during his first missionary journey (Acts 16:1-2). On the other hand, Acts also indicates that Paul evangelized "the Galatian country and Phrygia" (Acts 16:6) on a later missionary journey after returning to Syrian Antioch from Macedonia and Achaia (Acts 18:3). In Acts, Luke's tendency to avoid using Roman territorial designations in preference to local, ethnic ones would seemingly favor the northern territory over the southern, but then the issue of the sequence (or number) of Paul's missionary journeys arises. The northern territory, around the cities of Ancyra, Tavium, and Pessinus, was the traditional ethnic area of Galatia. Celts, the ethnic Galatians, had settled there since the third century BCE, though they clearly intermarried and moved around. The southern, "provincial" Galatia did not contain only ethnic Celts but had a diverse population centered in several cities, as mentioned in Acts 13—14. Many scholars tie the issue concerning the identity of the Galatians to the question of dating the letter, whether early or late in Paul's missionary career, but this may not be necessary. In any case, the letter was written after Paul's original evangelization of the Galatians, and the dating of the letter can be considered separately.

Clearly, Paul founded several Christian communities in Galatia (pl. "churches"), but he is not precise in identifying their location. Many scholars believe Paul evangelized the Galatians early in his missionary career after having successfully evangelized Cyprus, as Barnabas's understudy, and Perga and Antioch in Pisidia. In Acts (ch. 13), this missionary activity occurs before the Council of Jerusalem (Acts 15), where Paul's mission to the gentiles was confirmed by the authorities of the church, especially Cephas (Simon Peter) and James the brother of the Lord, both of whom are mentioned in Galatians in this context (2:7–14). Acts, however, portrays the mission to Galatia as occurring after the Council of Jerusalem (chs. 16, 18).

The letter does not resolve the issue either, though it helps identify the reason Paul wrote it. Paul's primary concern is that the Galatians, to whom he had preached the gospel, have quickly abandoned it under pressure from preachers from Jerusalem who have come, apparently with the backing of James the brother of the Lord, insisting on circumcision in order to follow Jesus. Essentially, they were demanding that gentile converts must become Jews, in other words, assume the requirements of the law, to be true followers of Jesus. This flies in the face of Paul's message and appears to have been a key item resolved at the Council of Jerusalem. After his conversion and call, Paul came to the realization that circumcision as a badge of religious identity was no longer a requirement for followers of Jesus, especially gentiles. Galatians is a strong defense of his message and a forceful repudiation of the pro-Jewish preachers from Jerusalem who evidently seduced the Galatians with their arguments.

Consequently, I join those scholars who hold that Paul wrote Galatians early in his missionary career (ca. 54–55 CE), but perhaps after the Council of Jerusalem and after having evangelized northern Galatia (ca. 50). He wrote perhaps from Ephesus, where he spent a long sojourn, and could easily have heard about the difficulties in his Galatian communities after having moved on to further missionary work, which was his custom. The following chart detailing the synopsis of Paul's life summarizes a plausible reconstruction of his life and ministry.

SYNOPSIS OF THE LIFE OF PAUL OF TARSUS		
EVENT	**DATE (CE)***	**SCRIPTURE**
Birth in Tarsus	1–10	None
Education in Tarsus and (?) Jerusalem Persecution of "the Way"	10–33	Gal 1:13–14; 1 Cor 15:9; Phil 3:6; Acts 8:1–3; 9:1–2
Conversion/commission/call near Damascus	33–35	Gal 1:15–16; Acts 9:1–19
Three years in Arabia (Nabataea?) and Damascus	36–38	Gal 1:17
Short visit to Jerusalem (Two weeks with "pillars" of the Church, Cephas and James the brother of the Lord)	35–38	Gal 1:18
Missionary activity in Cilicia, Galatia, Syria, Antioch	37–45	Gal 1:21; Acts 9:30
Paul and Barnabas in Cyprus and Anatolia	45–46	Acts 13:4—14:28
Council of Jerusalem	46-49	Gal 2:1–10; Acts 15:1–21 (Acts 11:1–18?)
Span of missionary activity in Asia Minor, Macedonia, etc. [*Period of extant letter writing*]	49–60	Acts 16—20
Paul and Silas/Silvanus in Macedonia and Achaia: Philippi, Thessalonica, Beroea	49–52	Acts 16:9—18:18
Sojourn in Corinth (18 months)†	50–52	Acts 18:1–18
Sojourn in Ephesus (2.5–3 yrs.)	52–56	Acts 19:1—20:1
Last visit to Jerusalem; arrest, imprisonment in Caesarea (2 yrs.)	56–59	Acts 21:15—26:32
Trial before Festus, voyage to Rome		Acts 23:35—26:32
Imprisonment and preaching in Rome (2 yrs.)	60–63	Acts 28:16–31
Martyrdom in Rome	62–64	None

* All dates are approximate; overlapping is based upon possible conflicting information and reconstructions.

† Appearance before Gallio in Corinth (50/51); date of the first letter of Paul, 1 Thessalonians, the earliest book in the New Testament.

LITERARY CHARACTERISTICS

Literarily, Galatians is one of Paul's most personal letters. It contains lengthy autobiographical sections, and its tone is filled with passion and palpable personal sentiment. On occasion, the reader gets the impression that Paul becomes almost overwhelmed with emotion as he dictates his letter. Some passages show evidence of the spontaneity of thought characteristic of someone in an intense debate. Another characteristic of the letter is the use of Jewish and Greco-Roman forms of argumentation. Paul is adept at both rabbinic interpretation and rhetorical refinement typical of the Greek-speaking world.

Ancient manuscript of Galatians (ca. 200 CE)

Thematically, Galatians is closely related to the Letter to the Romans, Paul's most detailed and profound explanation of his understanding of the Christian faith. Both letters expound on the themes of the law (torah), faith, righteousness (justification), salvation, life in the Spirit, and the meaning of true freedom. Galatians also emphasizes Paul's notion of "gospel," the importance of the cross, and the ethical characteristics of life in Christ.

The closeness of language between Romans and Galatians, and the fact that some of their themes are not emphasized in Paul's other letters, has led some scholars to presume the two were written in proximate sequence. But whereas Romans is almost certainly one of Paul's last letters, the one in which he developed most fully his theological vision, Galatians, as noted earlier, more likely represents Paul's early foray into the theological depth that would eventually make him famous.

THEOLOGY

Let me begin with an anecdote. When a French-speaking confrere from my community of priests, the Sulpicians, discovered my interest in Galatians, he asked me unexpectedly, "If Saint Paul were writing to the French today, what would be his principal themes?" Puzzled, I thought for a moment and then knowingly smiled and said in French, *Liberté, fraternité, égalité* (freedom, brotherhood/sisterhood, and equality). This is the motto of the French nation since the time of the French Revolution (1789), and these three interrelated themes are indeed characteristic of the theology of Galatians. Even more interesting is the fact that the ethnic background of the Galatians is distantly related to France. The ancestors of the Galatians came from Gaul as mercenaries and settled in what is now central Turkey. So, the theological message, ancient and modern, is unified.

No single letter of Paul, not even Romans, summarizes Paul's theology. The primary reason is that all of Paul's letters were occasional. They were written to specific audiences (individuals or groups), on specific occasions, and for specific reasons. Nevertheless, one can summarize the theological perspective of each letter from the viewpoint of its own emphases, the impact it likely had on the first readers, and its contemporary application.

Galatians provides a stellar example. Paul wrote to various churches in Galatia—perhaps only three or four small Christian communities—where he had evangelized and where all his hard work was beginning to dissipate because of outside preachers from Jerusalem who came to correct or reorient Paul's gospel message. Paul was emotionally invested in these communities. He considered them his spiritual children; even during his heated arguments with them, he holds on to this affection (see 4:19).

The issue with the Galatians was eminently pastoral as well as theological. Essentially, were they going to succumb to outside pressure to abandon the gospel message Paul and his companions had preached, and turn to the slavery of circumcision and the law? Paul writes forcefully to persuade them to come to their senses, to return to the "truth of the gospel" (2:3, 14). Paul musters all the necessary arguments to defend his gospel and to justify his strong exhortation to the Galatians to return to the proper path. First, he uses his own autobiographical story to show the extrahuman basis for his own apostolic call, thus affirming the divine origin of his message. Then, he emphasizes the contrast of faith and works of the law. True righteousness, he insists, comes from the faith of (and in) Christ and not from performing special "works," especially those tied to certain aspects of the Jewish law that had been connected to identity, namely, circumcision and the food laws. Paul insists that once one is baptized into Christ, one is a "new creation" (6:15; cf. 2 Cor 5:17). As such, prior requisites of the law no longer hold sway for those who come to the gospel of Jesus Christ. Given that his Galatian communities were gentile, this was a crucial teaching. For Paul, turning to circumcision was tantamount to voluntarily accepting slavery (4:8–11). In Christ, they had become free. Freedom from the law also meant freedom from the burdens and minutiae of the law. In Christ, they were called to live by the Holy Spirit and thus to live ethically upright lives that bore the fruit of this new life (5:22–26). Living by love rather than by conformity to prescriptions of the law is more fundamental in the new creation (5:14). Despite the lack of frequency of "new creation" language, in Paul's letters, I take it to be a fundamental concept in Paul's theology.

OVERVIEW

Before interpreting Galatians in detail, an overview of my approach may be helpful, especially for those who want a preview or summary. The occasion of the letter is clearly the controversy that has erupted in the Galatian communities founded by Paul because of some outside agitators, apparently closely allied to James the brother of the Lord in Jerusalem. In Paul's absence they have come to the Galatians, all gentiles, to persuade them that they must become Jews to follow Jesus Christ. This position runs absolutely counter to Paul's teaching. So, when he hears about it, he is furious and dictates the letter to set the record straight and to call his communities back to the "truth of the gospel."

Regarding content, the letter revolves around eight distinct but interrelated themes. The primary theme—although only mentioned once explicitly, and at the end of the letter (6:15)—is *new creation*. In Galatians, Paul is calling them back to the realization that his gospel message led them to a new life in Jesus Christ, one that no longer required the fulfillment of certain aspects of the law that would bestow upon them a chosen identity as God's favored people. In *baptism*, they have already begun the life in the new creation. They have already been made new through God's *grace*! They thus no longer need the supports that come from Jewish identity, such as circumcision and the dietary laws. What has brought about this dramatic transformation is the *cross* and resurrection. Through Jesus's action of accepting death on the cross, and thereby accomplishing his Father's will and being vindicated in the resurrection by the Father, the Galatians have become true children of the Father, true heirs of their heavenly destiny. Jesus's death on a cross is what made salvation possible in all its attendant concepts, including *justification* by faith. Jesus's own *faith*, understood as fidelity to his Father's will, has made it possible for the Galatians to live in *freedom* and to tie their *faith in* Christ to his faithful actions. This life in the new creation entails no less than living in accordance with the *Spirit* and avoiding the attractions of the "flesh." There is a strong ethical dimension to life in the new creation. Paul insists that the Galatians not fall into slavery now that they have become free sons and daughters of God. Living in accordance with this freedom, however, means not only rejecting the seduction of the agitators but also living the law of love, as Jesus taught, and as is evident in the ethical contrast between Spirit and flesh, so foundational to Paul's ethical perspective influenced by his apocalyptic outlook. Moreover, Paul dramatically draws attention to another dimension of life in the new creation. Typical human divisions fall away. There can be no more distinction between Jew or gentile, slave or free, male and female. All are one in Christ; all are heirs of the same promise.

This summary of a complex letter shows the essence of my approach. In these eight themes—new creation, baptism, the cross, justification, faith, freedom, grace, the Spirit—Paul's message forcefully calls on the Galatians to remain faithful to God's call they have received through Paul's preaching and to resist steadfastly the enticements to retreat into a new form of slavery that does not befit the children of God. All this has been made possible by God's grace, which Paul believes is still acting in their lives and will perhaps ultimately entice them to come to their senses. The clarion call to freedom has struck a chord throughout the history of interpretation of Galatians. Its message is as pertinent today as ever it was, especially in modern contexts where freedom is sometimes confused with unbridled licentiousness. Consequently, it is worth exploring this letter in greater detail, which is the goal of this spiritual-pastoral commentary. Life in the new creation may not be easy—either to live or to understand—but it is the precious gift we have been given in Christ Jesus.

Saint Augustine's Interpretation

Saint Augustine (354–430 CE) is one of the outstanding early interpreters of Paul's letters. Here is his explanation of why Paul wrote Galatians:

> The reason the Apostle writes to the Galatians is so they may understand what it is that God's grace accomplishes for them: they are no longer under the law. For though the grace of the gospel had been preached to them, there were some from the circumcision who still did not grasp the real benefit of grace. Despite being called Christians, they still wanted to be under the burdens of a law—burdens that the Lord God had imposed not on those serving righteousness but on those serving sin. That is, he had given a righteous law to unrighteous people to point out their sins, not take them away. He takes away sins only by the grace of *faith, which works through love* (Gal 5:6).
>
> So then, these people wanted to put the Galatians, who were already under this grace, under the burdens of the law, claiming that the gospel would be of no benefit to them unless they were circumcised and submitted to other carnal observances of Jewish custom. Because of this claim, the Galatians had begun to regard the apostle Paul, who had preached the gospel to them, as suspect on the ground that he did not hold the teaching of the other apostles, who were compelling Gentiles to live like Jews. To avoid scandalizing such people, the apostle Peter had yielded to them and had thus been led into hypocrisy (Lat. *simulatio*), as though he too believed that the

gospel was of no benefit to Gentiles unless they fulfilled the burdens of the law. The apostle Paul calls him back from this hypocrisy, as he demonstrates in this very letter.

The point at issue in the Letter to the Romans is similar, but with this apparent difference: there he resolves an actual conflict, settling a dispute that had arisen between believers of Jewish and Gentile origin. (Plumer, 125.)

Getting the full picture of the issues in Galatians is a challenge, since we have only one half of the conversation, namely Paul's. Missing is the precise argumentation of his opponents. Since they likely used numerous OT passages to bolster their argumentation, Paul also delves into his vast storehouse of knowledge of the Hebrew Scriptures (in their Greek form, the Septuagint) to strengthen his own position. His primary resource is the Genesis story of Abraham, whom Paul views as *the* model of faith because of his immediate acceptance of God's will (3:6–9; cf. Gen 15:6; Rom 4:1–9). Abraham is Paul's ideal, the model of a free person, the opposite of someone tied to the law and its requirements. Through a lengthy and complex analogy based on Abraham's two wives, Paul shows that the Galatians are truly children of the "free" woman and not the slave (4:21–31). If one is free in Christ, then one cannot assume the slavery of practices associated with the law. When one is marked with the sign of the cross, one cannot simply abandon it. Indeed, Paul's argument in Galatians is strongly based on the power of the cross of Christ. The message Paul preached, and the very life he led, was always rooted in this scandalous reality that Jesus was crucified. In the eyes of the world, Paul knows that this is folly (see 1 Cor 1:23). It is also at the center of his gospel message. One cannot preach an "easy" Christianity. Being an authentic follower of the true gospel means accepting the burdens of this paradoxical message. The cross wrought salvation and marks the identity of all Christians in the world.

Who Were Paul's Opponents in Galatia?

This question is difficult to answer since we have no real identifying features nor written information from them. Their arguments are surmised from reading "between the lines" of Galatians. Paul is vague, calling them "false believers" (2:4 *pseudadelphous*, lit. "false brothers"), or "certain people [who] came from James" (2:12), and obviously seeing them as disturbers of the community (1:7; 5:10). Clearly they were Jewish Christians who were still tied to the Mosaic torah and who insisted that gentile converts adhere to the law as well, especially concerning circumcision and dietary regulations, which were important identifying features in Judaism. Whether Paul may have accurately depicted their message or perhaps exaggerated it in the heat of argument, he clearly perceives them as opponents to his gospel message and disturbers of the peace for his Galatians.

Traditionally, scholars called these opponents "Judaizers" on the basis of the verb used in 2:14 (*ioudaïzō*, "live like a Jew"). But "Judaizers" is not the best term here because it normally refers to gentiles who favor Jewish customs (LXX, Josephus), whereas Paul's opponents are Jewish followers of the Jesus movement promoting Jewish practices. Other terms have become more current: false teachers or evangelizers, new preachers, troublemakers, disturbers, and agitators. This commentary will use the term *agitators* because it highlights the disturbing characteristics of their alternative "gospel" while not narrowly focusing on circumcision. More is at stake. Their message goes against Paul's entire understanding of the "new creation" that the Christ event has brought about.

Whether Paul's arguments ultimately swayed the Galatians to abandon their folly, we cannot be certain. In his perplexity and frustration, Paul seems almost resigned to the possibility that his letter may fall on deaf ears (4:11, 20). Yet we know that it made enough of an impact to be preserved in the Pauline corpus. Throughout the history of exegesis, Galatians has been one of the more influential letters of Paul, significantly contributing to Pauline theology through the ages (see Riches, *Galatians*).

OUTLINE

Most of Paul's letters can be outlined with a similar fourfold pattern that follows a standard letter format from the Greco-Roman world: Greeting, Thanksgiving, Body, Closing. Furthermore, Paul's letters often have extensive sections of ethical teaching, formally called paraenesis. Paul usually includes this teaching in the body of the letter as a way of incorporating dramatic exhortations in his argumentation. In addition, Paul's letters often contain information about his or his companions' travel plans.

The Letter to the Galatians generally follows this standard format with one major exception. There is no thanksgiving! Scholars debate the precise reason(s) for this lack, but the content of the letter indicates that Paul is highly upset with the Galatians and their abandonment of his gospel message (3:1). It is quite likely that Paul deliberately leaves out this customary section of the letter, both to signal his pique and to launch right into his argument.

On the question of outline, mention must also be made of a modern proposal by some scholars (especially Betz) to emphasize the rhetorical nature of the letter in accord with Greco-Roman rules of rhetoric. Such scholars thus propose to classify Galatians in one or another form of the three main types of rhetoric: forensic (or judicial), deliberative (or hortatory), or epideictic (or demonstrative). Forensic rhetoric tries to persuade people about past events; deliberative tries to persuade people to take a certain course of action; epideictic tries to affirm and defend certain points of view in the present. The problem with such proposals is the lack of unity among scholars and the fact that Galatians cannot easily be categorized into any one form proposed. Clearly, Paul used rhetorical argumentation in the letter. He was familiar with some techniques of ancient rhetoric. But classifying the letter as one type of rhetorical letter or another would be unwise. It is better to acknowledge the presence of some rhetorical elements in the letter, which Paul fashioned in accordance with his custom into a friendly but challenging letter to a community that he had founded and loved.

As with all NT documents, scholars have proposed many different detailed outlines of the letter. The following outline accounts for Paul's complex argumentation as well as the typical flow of a Pauline letter.

I.   Greeting (1:1–5)

II. Fidelity to the Gospel (1:6–10)
     Paul's Amazement at the Galatians (1:6–9)
     Contrast of Human and Divine (1:10)

III. Paul's Defense of the Gospel and His Authority (1:11—2:21)
     Origin of the Gospel (1:11–12)
     Paul's Autobiographical Story (1:13–24)
     Paul's Version of the Council of Jerusalem (2:1–10)
     Paul's Confrontation of Peter at Antioch (2:11–14)
     Theme of the Letter: Faith and Works (2:15–21)

IV. Faith and Freedom (3:1—4:31)
     Justification by Faith and the Figure of Abraham (3:1–14)
     The Law and the Promise (3:15–22)
     What Faith Has Brought (3:23–29)
     Heirs, Not Slaves (4:1–11)
     Paul's Plea to the Galatians (4:12–20)
     An Allegory on Christian Freedom (4:21–31)

V.   Exhortation to Christian Living (5:1—6:10)
     Faith and Freedom (5:1–6)
     Paul's Further Plea to the Galatians (5:7–12)
     Freedom for Service and the Contrast between Flesh and Spirit (5:13–26)
     Life in the Community of Christ (6:1–10)

VI. Closing (6:11–18)
     Paul's Final Plea (6:11–17)
     Final Greeting (6:18)

1
THE GREETING (1:1–5)

Galatians is a letter born of controversy. It begins with a rather standard Pauline greeting (1:1–15), but the tone quickly changes. Paul skips the "thanksgiving" section that was customary in his letters. Instead, he immediately addresses the question at hand—his dismay at the Galatians' abandonment, under pressure, of his gospel message (1:6–10).

> **1** [1] Paul an apostle—not from human beings nor by human authority, but through Jesus Christ and God the Father, who raised him from the dead— [2] and all the brothers and sisters who are with me, to the churches of Galatia: [3] Grace to you and peace from God the Father and our Lord Jesus Christ, [4] who gave himself for our sins in order to rescue us from the present evil age, according to the will of our God and Father, [5] to whom be glory forever and ever. Amen.

These five verses constitute the greeting of the Letter to the Galatians. All of Paul's letters in the New Testament begin with an opening greeting, and all mention his name, Paul. Most greetings are terse and to the point, providing the name of the sender(s), the name of the recipient(s), and some formal greetings. This opening of seventy-five Greek words is the second longest of the thirteen letters in the Pauline corpus after Romans, which has ninety-three words. Initially, one would assume that these verses are merely a formality. In fact, they are more important than a standard formula. Virtually every word is packed with meaning and sets forth Paul's larger agenda in the letter, namely, a defense of his apostolic proclamation of the gospel of Jesus Christ.

In accord with the standard Greco-Roman letter and typical Pauline practice, the greeting can be outlined in three sections:

(1) identification of the sender (vv. 1–2a);
(2) identification of the receivers (v. 2b); and
(3) greeting and prayerful wishes (vv. 3–5).

Letters in the Bible

For similar greetings in Paul's letters, see Rom 1:1-7; 1 Cor 1:1-3; 2 Cor 1:1-2; Phil 1:1-2; 1 Thess 1:1; and Phlm 1-3. The length of a letter does not necessarily affect the length of the greeting. Philemon, Paul's shortest letter, contains a forty-one-word greeting. First Thessalonians, with nineteen words, has the shortest. Importantly, in the Pauline letters, the greetings are not merely formalities; they hint at important themes to come.

No book of the OT is in the form of a letter, although letters are mentioned several times (2 Sam 11:15; 2 Kgs 5:5-6; Ezra 4:7-23). The Catholic canon of Scripture preserves the so-called letter of Jeremiah—actually, more a sermon composed later in Jeremiah's name—which is included at the end of the Book of Baruch (6:1-73) in the Vulgate form. Twenty-one (of twenty-seven) books of the NT are in letter format; thirteen of these in Paul's name. Obviously, the letter was a very important form of communication in the early Church (see also the seven letters in Rev 1:4–3:22).

Letters in Antiquity

The letter form is as old as human writing. Archaeologists have found many examples of letters in various ancient languages written, for instance, on clay tablets, shards of pottery (called ostraca), and animal skins. Many Greek letters written on papyrus were found in Egypt, and these have helped scholars better understand the NT background.

In comparison to many letters in antiquity, Paul's letters are very long. The famous Roman orator Cicero, for example, wrote many letters, most of which numbered barely 300 words. Many personal letters averaged less than 100 words. By contrast, Paul's letters average about 1,300 words, with Romans being more than 7,000! Often letter writers used the services of a trained scribe, someone who could professionally read and write (see Paul's mention of Tertius, Rom 16:22), although scholars now know that literacy was more widespread in the Greco-Roman world than originally thought.

The Greco-Roman world also possessed handbooks describing letter writing and identifying various types of letters. To name a few: friendly, congratulatory, exhortatory, apologetic, and consoling. Letters in the NT seemingly defy absolute categorization, and Paul evidently used rhetorical devices from various types of letters.

Unlike modern postal services, the average person in antiquity had to send correspondence by couriers, whether friends, acquaintances, or merchants and the like, who were traveling to the desired destination. Postal services existed in antiquity since the Persian Empire, but these were restricted to military and government officials. Some of Paul's couriers included Titus (2 Cor 8:16-18), Epaphroditus (Phil 2:25-28), and Phoebe (Rom 16:1-2).

The first verse of the letter identifies "Paul" as the sender or primary author. This name, which in Latin means "little" and may refer to his physical stature (cf. 2 Cor 10:10), is the way Paul was known by his gentile[1] communities. In Jewish circles, Paul was more likely addressed by his Jewish name Saul.[2] More important, however, is how he describes himself. He takes great care to note that he is an "apostle." So, he is one who has been sent by God for a special mission. He makes his point emphatically with two negatively phrased expressions. His designation as an apostle comes "not from human beings nor by human authority." Here, Paul uses two different prepositions with a slightly nuanced meaning. The first emphasizes the origin of Paul's call; it did not come *from* human beings (cf. 1 Thess 2:6). His apostleship is not merely a human call to a specific position or function. The second preposition emphasizes the agency of his call as an apostle; it did not come *through* or *by means of* any human person, unlike others who were commissioned by congregations or individuals (cf. Phil 2:25; 2 Cor 8:23; 1 Tim 1:18). Both expressions clearly deny the human origin of Paul's call as an apostle, and by extension, indicate the divine origin of his call. Indeed, as is clear throughout all of Paul's letters, the designation as an apostle is of utmost importance (cf. 1 Cor 12:28), especially in this letter.

In these verses, Paul is at pains to deny the human origin of his call. As he goes on to explain, his call as an apostle came "through Jesus Christ and God the Father, who raised him from the dead." This statement constitutes the positive assertion that contrasts with the double denial expressed in the earlier phrase. Paul was called to his apostleship by Jesus Christ and God the Father. In other words, Paul's apostleship is of no less divine origin than those who were before him as apostles, primarily the Twelve (1 Cor 15:9–10), who were appointed by Jesus during his lifetime.

Paul's Apostleship

Saint Augustine comments on Paul's apostleship being equal to the Twelve: "Thus the earlier apostles, who were sent not from human beings but by God through a human being—that is, through Jesus Christ while he was still mortal— were truthful. And the last apostle, who was sent by Jesus Christ now wholly God after his resurrection, is also truthful….The authority of Paul's witness should therefore be regarded as equal to theirs." (Plumer, 127, 129)

As will be seen later in the letter, this assertion is of prime importance for Paul, for his apostleship has been called into question by certain agitators who have offered the Galatians an alternative gospel message. It is also noteworthy that this verse contains the only explicit mention in Galatians of the resurrection of Jesus, although there are hints of it elsewhere.[3] Although Paul talks at length elsewhere about the resurrection (1 Cor 15; Rom 1:4; 10:9; 2 Cor 4:14; Phil 3:10), it is not center stage in Galatians. Here, it appears at the beginning of the letter to underline subtly Paul's commission as a disciple by the *risen* Lord himself (cf. Gal 1:12; Acts 9:4–5).

Paul as an Apostle

Paul's apostleship is at the center of the issues in Galatians, not for its own sake, but because it is the authoritative foundation of his message. All of Paul's letters reflect the importance of this role. Paul uses the term *apostle* as a self-designation at the beginning of most of his letters (Rom 1:1; 1 Cor 1:1; 2 Cor 1:1; Eph 1:1; Col 1:1). In addition, when he names diverse ministries in the Christian community, apostleship tops the list (cf. 1 Cor 12:28; see also Eph 3:5; 4:11). The designation is rooted in Jesus's choosing twelve apostles for the mission of proclaiming the good news of salvation (Mark 3:14; 16:15; Matt 10:2; 28:16-20; Luke 6:13; Acts 1:2). The Greek root (*apostellō*) means to "send out." Apostles are sent on missions. The word is not used with this special meaning of being sent on a mission to proclaim a religious message in the OT or in secular Greek literature of Paul's day. Paul acknowledges other types of "apostles" (the Twelve, the "super-apostles"), but his identification is a calling by the Lord, such as a prophet is set apart for mission (cf. Gal 1:15). Paul's insistence that he too has been sent on a mission, albeit from the *risen* Lord Jesus Christ (1 Cor 15:8-11; Acts 9:15; 26:16-17), serves as the foundation of his ministry.

The second verse contributes further to the identity of the senders and the recipients. The expression "all the brothers and sisters" does not allow us to identify exactly who else is with Paul at the time, although the descriptive "all" may help lend authority to Paul's letter.[4] The identity of these individuals would depend largely on the origin and date of the letter (see introduction). If Paul is sending the letter from Ephesus, for example, then perhaps he is in the company of colleagues such as Timothy or Titus. It is also possible that Paul is in the company of other missionaries who had evangelized with him in Galatia.[5] Although contemporary readers identify Paul as the writer of all the letters that bear his name, many of his letters name others as "cosenders" with him, such as Sosthenes, Timothy, or Silvanus.[6] These are not necessarily to be identified with Paul's amanuenses, or scribes, to whom he dictated his letters (like Tertius in Rom 16:22), but trusted colleagues or coworkers.

The intended recipients of the letter are similarly identified with a vague expression, "the churches of Galatia" (see also 1 Cor 16:1; Acts 16:6; 18:23). (For the geographic identification of Galatia, see the introduction.) Paul regularly uses the singular "church" to designate an individual community of believers. Here, the use of the plural form indicates several small communities of believers founded by Paul and scattered in various towns throughout the region. He writes to all of them, indicating the letter is intended to be circulated among them for their instruction (see also 1 Thess 4:27).

The Church and the "Churches"

The word *church* (*ekklēsia*, from Greek "to call out of") originally meant an assembly or gathering of a group of people. The underlying biblical concept comes from the Hebrew *qahal* (assembly). Modern readers should not think of a church building, such as evolved later in the Church's history. In Paul's day, these communities of believers gathered in house churches. Paul's communities included numerous wealthy individuals whose private homes became the meeting place for the community (Rom 16:5; 1 Cor 16:19; Phlm 2). Paul acknowledges many groups of churches. Thus, he refers to the "churches of Asia" (1 Cor 16:19), "the churches of Judea" (Gal 1:22), or even "the churches of God" or "of Christ" (Rom 16:16; 1 Cor 11:16).

Yet rooted in the Pauline notion of church is also a universal conception that would emerge in later Pauline letters and in the Christian tradition (e.g., Eph 5:25-32). The seeds of this universal notion of "the Church" can be found already in Paul, for instance, in the expression, "the church of God" (1 Cor 1:2; 10:32; Gal 1:13). Not only are all the churches united in their belief in Jesus Christ as God's Son and universal Savior, but the Church as the "body of Christ" (cf. 1 Cor 12:27; Eph 4:12; 5:23) is intended to be one. For Paul, then, the churches exist as part of the great entity of the elect, the Church.

The final three verses of the greeting (vv. 3–5) express a typically Pauline sentiment accompanied by a prayerful wish. The dual notions of "grace and peace" are a regular feature of Paul's letters and are found elsewhere in the NT (cf. 1 Pet 1:2; 2 Pet 1:2; 2 John 1:3; Rev 1:4). "Grace" (*charis*)[7] used as a greeting, either at the beginning or end of letters (Gal 6:18; Rom 1:7; 16:20; etc.), is reminiscent of the typical Hellenistic greeting (*chairein*), but for Paul, it is even more significant, as we will see later. It recalls the gracious power of God at work in the world and especially in the life of the Church. This greeting is complemented by the expression of "peace," which translates the solemn Hebrew greeting of *shalōm* that to this day is used as a greeting (coming or going) among Jews. The wish of peace envisioned by this expression is not a bland, casual greeting but a profound wish for well-being upon the individual(s) receiving the greeting. In this simple, dual expression, Paul embodies the intercultural Hellenistic and Jewish environment in which he lived.

Grace and Peace

The Roman Catholic liturgy regularly incorporates words and phrases from the Bible in its standard formulae. Paul's traditional twofold greeting of "grace and peace" is often used at the beginning of the Mass in one or another formula of greeting, such as, "Grace to you and peace from God our Father and the Lord Jesus Christ." The Mass also adopts the early Christian greeting of peace or a "holy kiss" reflected in the Pauline letters (cf. Rom 16:16; 1 Cor 16:20; 2 Cor 13:12; 1 Thess 5:26) at the sharing of the "kiss of peace," which was reintroduced as part of the post–Vatican II liturgy. As with Paul's greetings, this kiss of peace is not an imitation of a secular "How are you?" but a heartfelt desire for well-being and blessing. It is a sign of the unity and love of all who are in the "body of Christ," which the Eucharist both signifies and brings about.

The identification of "God our Father and the Lord Jesus Christ"[8] is typically a Pauline expression of the origin of the divine action witnessed in the world (cf. Rom 1:7; 1 Cor 1:3; 2 Cor 1:2; Phlm 3). While it is not clear whether Paul conceives of God the Father and the Lord Jesus Christ as equally divine—scholars are sharply divided on this point—what is clear is that both are intimately implicated in Paul's message. For Paul, especially in the context of this letter, acknowledging God as Father (twice, vv. 1, 3) is equally to acknowledge the Galatians' identity as children of God (3:26; 4:6, 28, 31). The title "Lord," Paul's favorite title for Jesus, also emphasizes the unique role played by Jesus as Messiah in the Pauline communities: he is the risen Lord of the universe!

Note that Paul does not mention the Holy Spirit every time he mentions the Father and the Son. In Paul's day, the understanding of the Trinity as it would later develop in Christian thought was only just beginning. Paul's notion of the Spirit, in fact, is well developed elsewhere (cf. Rom 8:1–27). It also serves an important role in Galatians, especially in conjunction with the contrast with the law of Moses or torah (cf. Gal 3:2, 5; 5:17). Trinitarian formulae and understandings were still in flux, although the seeds of true Trinitarian thought are found in Paul (cf. 2 Cor 13:13).

The descriptive phrase about Jesus Christ, "who gave himself for our sins that he might rescue us from the present evil age in accord with the will of our God and Father" reveals three essential facts that Paul emphasizes in accordance with his gospel message. First, Jesus freely died *for* our sins in order to rescue us. This is critical to his understanding of the salvific effect of Jesus's life, death, and resurrection (see also 1 Tim 2:6). Second, this act of salvation is to save us "from the present evil age." This statement harbors an unspoken adjunct assertion: there will be a glorious age to come. It is part of the NT's apocalyptic outlook, a contrasting vision of the past and present era (of sin) and the future era (of salvation) that has already begun in Jesus Christ. Third, all this happened and continues to be effective "according to the will" of God. Jesus's gracious act of offering his own life for the sake of salvation is all part of God's marvelous plan for saving humanity from its sinfulness.

The Two Ages

Paul's use of the expression "the present evil age" calls for comment. The early Christians were much influenced by apocalyptic thought, the expectation that had developed in late Judaism that God would act definitively in human history to bring about a totally new world. Paul, reflecting such apocalyptic belief, sets up a sharp contrast between "the present evil age" and the future age to come (see also Heb 6:5). Essentially, he believed in two diametrically opposed eras: one distorted by the force of evil, and another dominated by good. His language about "this age" (Gk. *aiōn*, "age, era"; see 1 Cor 1:20; 2:6, 8; 3:18; cf. 2 Cor 4:4; Rom 12:2) reflects his belief in the passing value of this age in comparison to the age to come, another expression for the "new creation" (Gal 6:15).

The basis for this belief likely goes back to the teaching of Jesus of Nazareth. The Gospels record his oral teaching about "this age" in contrast to "the age to come" (Mark 10:30; Matt 12:32; Luke 18:30). The OT, itself, provided some of the background for this contrast, as some of the prophets distinguished between the present evil and future glory (Isa 43:18–19), and some of the OT apocrypha similarly contrast two ages (4 Ezra 2:36, 39; 4:6–7).

Several aspects of Paul's threefold assertion are noteworthy. Unusually here, he uses the plural "sins" (*harmartiōn*) rather than his customary expression "sin" (fifty-nine times), which identifies it as a singular force in human existence that is opposed to all that is good. The wording may represent an early Christian creedal statement, rooted in the liturgy, concerning the atoning effect of Jesus's death (e.g., 1 Cor 15:3; see Col 1:14). It might thus lend some emphasis to the authoritative nature of Paul's message.

Another interesting fact is Paul's use of the verb *rescue* (*exaireō*, to "tear out, remove"). The NT does not use the word often, but here, Paul employs it to great effect to emphasize that Jesus's self-donation for our sake was to snatch us out of harm's way.[9] Jesus acts on our behalf.[10] This powerful statement underlines Paul's insistence later in the letter that the gift of salvation, which the Galatians have received in Jesus Christ, is a freeing one (Gal 5:1). They have no need to seek other means to escape the evils of this age. The expression "the present evil age" (see Rom 12:2; 1 Cor 2:6, 8; Eph 5:16) obviously implies the existence of an alternative: the age to come, which is a key element in Paul's eschatology, his view of the "end times," when God's ultimate victory over sin and evil will be permanently established at Jesus's return in glory (1 Thess 5:1–3; Eph 1:21).

Finally, Paul concludes the opening of his letter with a doxology, a prayer giving "glory" to God, which may originate in a liturgical setting. In typical Jewish fashion, Paul includes the Hebrew word "Amen," the word of assent that normally concluded Jewish prayers and that Paul adds here as a virtual exclamation mark on his opening salvo of what will be a tough conversation with his beloved but errant Galatians. While it is not unusual for Paul to interject prayers within his letters, and indeed in the middle of serious discussions, these are usually found later in the body of his letters rather than at the beginning.[11] A prayerful liturgical wish in this opening helps Paul stay focused on God amid his agitation at the Galatians' abandonment of the gospel. Moreover, it reminds the Galatians of the larger context of their faith, expressed in worship and praise of God, right before Paul launches a direct assault on their presumption.

Amen at the Beginning Rather than the End?

Saint John Chrysostom (349-407 CE) is one of the most important commentators on Paul's letters from the patristic era. He was patriarch of Constantinople and reputed to be a great homilist, for which he was later called "golden mouth" (Chrysostom), which became his surname. He comments on Paul's use of Amen:

> We nowhere find the word *amen* placed at the beginning or in the prologue of his [Paul's] letters but after many words. But here, showing that what he has said is a sufficient accusation of the Galatians and that the argument is closed, he made this the prologue. For it does not take long to establish charges that are patently true….But not only for this reason does he do it but because he is exceedingly astonished by the magnitude of the gift, the excess of grace and what God did at once in a tiny space of time for those in such a state. Unable to express this in words, Paul breaks into a doxology. (Chrysostom, 1.5)

PASTORAL AND SPIRITUAL OBSERVATIONS

This greeting of Paul that opens his letter to the Galatians is not merely a formula. It is rich in deep theological insight. The contemporary liturgical use of the first two verses of the passage, used in conjunction with verses 6–10, sets the proper context for understanding these seemingly simple verses. They are foundational to Paul's essential message in the entire letter. Although he uses literary convention in opening the letter with typical greetings, his message is more profound. He defends his apostleship with striking force, emphasizing its divine origin from the risen Lord Jesus himself, under God's authority, and thus repudiating any minimalization of it that was either implied or explicitly stated by the agitators who were opposed to Paul's gospel. It is paradoxical that Paul would have to defend his apostleship so forcefully, for later Christian tradition identified him as *the* apostle par excellence, and he was always known as "apostle to the gentiles" (Rom 11:13; see Acts 22:21; 26:20).

Christ founded the Church on the apostles, and Paul is proud to count his apostleship as equal to those who had received their call from Jesus during his earthly lifetime. In a sense, Paul's position is fortuitous for all later Christians. Our call to continue the work of the apostolic Church is rooted in the ongoing work of the risen Lord Jesus. Today, he continues to call forth and commission apostles, workers to carry forth his message of salvation in the world.

Christ's obedience, which is often noted in the NT (e.g., Matt 26:42; Luke 22:42; John 8:29; Heb 10:7), is enshrined also in the prayer he taught his disciples: "your will be done, on earth as it is in heaven" (Matt 6:10), part of the prayer Christians pray daily, which we call "the Lord's Prayer." Apostleship is an invitation to follow Jesus in doing the will of God. Paul uses this notion as part of his christological affirmation: Christ's offering of himself was done in fulfillment of God's will, the divine plan of salvation. It also subtly recalls that doing God's will and not our own is essentially what faith is. Paul reminds the Galatians of this dynamic by placing his greeting on a solid foundation with the example of Christ himself.

What is masterful about this brief opening to the letter is Paul's dual use of the material. On the one hand, he greets the Galatians cordially and with (already) traditional Christian formulae that root his message in God's action in Jesus Christ. He affirms his coworkers and the apostolic tradition they uphold. Yet subtly, at the same time, he sets the Galatians up to receive a stern message that will be hard for them to accept. One commentator puts it succinctly: "For a brief moment, having warmly embraced the coworkers who are present with him as he writes the letter, he holds the Galatians at arm's length" (Martyn, 86). It is Paul at his best, ever faithful to his apostolic calling and ever vigilant to ensure that his communities do not stray from the truth of the message he imparted to them as an apostle.

This little passage can serve as a potent reminder in our own day that the message with which we are entrusted is not our own. This is especially true for those called to preach the gospel formally, such as those in ordained ministries. To be truly apostolic is to be rooted in and faithful to the gospel message as received and proclaimed throughout history. To do otherwise is to risk the very thing Paul accused the Galatians of doing: abandoning "the truth of the gospel" (Gal 2:5, 14).

REFLECTION QUESTIONS

1. Why is being an apostle the most important aspect of Paul's identity as a follower of Jesus? Do you see any ramifications of his idea for us today?

2. How do you understand the greeting of "grace and peace"? What comparable sentiments might be used today to greet someone in a letter?

3. Paul insists firmly that his message—the gospel—is not of human origin but is divine. How can one prove such a claim? How might the Galatians have reacted to it?

4. What do you make of the contrast between the two ages, the present "evil" age and the age to come? Do you believe in this stark division? How is one to survive the present age to make it to the other?

5. What is the role of prayer in your own life, especially regarding debates or arguments? How easy is it to remain prayerful amid sharp disagreements?

2

FIDELITY TO THE GOSPEL (1:6–10)

After the greeting, Paul launches immediately into the crux of the matter, without the customary thanksgiving section found in his other letters.[1] The body of the letter begins here, and Paul states in stark terms the essential problem. He is extremely upset because the Galatians have quickly abandoned the gospel he preached to them. In three quick strokes, he lays out his accusation. In the first section (vv. 6–7), he charges them with forsaking the gospel. He follows this with a double invocation of a curse upon anyone who preaches a false gospel (vv. 8–9). Finally, he asks rhetorically whether the Galatians understand his true motivation (v. 10). Do they think he is merely trying to please human beings? He answers his own question by invoking one of his favorite self-designations: he is a "slave of Christ." He works to please his Divine Master, not any human beings.

> [6] I am astonished that you are turning away so quickly from the one who called you in the grace of Christ for a different gospel— [7] not that there is another one— but there are some people who are disturbing you and wanting to pervert the gospel of Christ. [8] But even if we or an angel from heaven should proclaim to you a gospel contrary to the one we proclaimed to you, let that person be accursed! [9] As we said before, and now I say again, if anyone proclaims to you a gospel contrary to what you have received, let that person be accursed! [10] For, am I now appealing to human beings, or to God? Or am I trying to please human beings? If I were still trying to please human beings, I would not be a slave of Christ.

Cf. 1 Cor 15:1–2; 16:22; 2 Cor 11:1–6; 1 Thess 2:1–8; 2 Thess 2:15.

One can almost hear the astonishment in Paul's voice as he fervently launches his argument. He is "amazed" at how readily they have deserted him and his message. The verb is often used in the Gospels for reaction to Jesus's great deeds or miracles. Paul rarely employs the word, and its presence in this context indicates his surprise, perhaps as much at the speed at which they are "forsaking" (NRSV "deserting") the gospel he preached. That the Galatians have abandoned both the message and, by implication, the bearer of the message and their spiritual "parent"—Paul—is clear. But he is particularly incensed because their actions reveal a deeper betrayal. They are forsaking "the one who called you by [the] grace [of Christ]," that is, God, who was the true source of their call. All that Paul had done in his evangelization had been accomplished by the grace (or power) of Christ, who was both the force behind the message and its principal content. Paul was but its servant ("slave," v. 10).

To describe those who are "disturbing you," Paul uses a participle in the plural form (*tarassontes*; NJB "trouble-makers") that later in the letter is used in the singular form (5:10), but probably in the sense of a generic group of agitators. One of the great challenges in Galatians is determining the identity of these opponents of Paul (see introduction). Although Paul faced opposition elsewhere in his ministry, there is no reason to identify these agitators with other regions (e.g., the "super-apostles" in 2 Cor 11:5; 12:11). Acts indicates that Paul and his companions sometimes faced opposition in their ministry in other contexts (Acts 15:24), but this is the only letter where Paul employs this term. Elsewhere in the Bible, the term is often used in the metaphorical sense of being inwardly troubled (Pss 54:5; 108:22 LXX; John 14:1, 27), but Paul means it in the sense of causing trouble, agitating others, or purposefully misleading them.[2]

Paul's assertion that they "pervert the gospel of Christ" demonstrates how strongly he feels about their subversive activity.[3] For Paul, the interchangeable terms "gospel of Christ," "gospel of God," or "the gospel"[4] sum up the main message he imparted by his preaching: Jesus Christ accomplished God's will and saved humanity by his cross and resurrection in such a manner that strict observance of the torah is no longer necessary for Paul's gentile converts. These troublemakers are corrupting the very message Paul delivered for their benefit. Accepting another "gospel" is not an option. Paul, perhaps with sarcasm in his voice, remarks as an aside, "not that there is another." The gospel is indeed singular in the fullest sense of that word. There is only one message of salvation; there is only one Messiah, Jesus Christ and him crucified (Gal 3:1; 1 Cor 1:22–23; 2:2).

The Danger of Perverting the Gospel

The early Church fathers comment on the seriousness of Paul's charge against the Galatians in various ways. The concern was not only that turning from the true gospel and reverting to the torah would corrupt the faith but also would put in jeopardy the entire message. Two comments are exemplary of the concern:

Just as with royal currency—anyone who cuts off a little from the impress has debased the whole currency—so one who makes even the smallest change in sound faith adulterates the whole. (Theodore of Mopsuestia [ca. 350–428 CE], *CGPEP* 6:16)

No one should be surprised that the apostle, who was known for taming wild behavior, should have been so worked up about this, because it was for the sake of the Galatians' salvation that he was so angry with the enemies of Christian discipline. This very anger shows that it was a serious sin to turn back to the law after having received the faith. (Ambrosiaster [fourth cent. CE], 1.9.1, p. 4)

Paul then repeats his message in stronger terms. If anyone, even "an angel from heaven" (i.e., a divine messenger!) offers the Galatians an alternative gospel message, "let that one be accursed [*anathema estō*]." Paul's invocation of a curse is strong, but sometimes Paul felt so strongly about such matters that he could use colorful and highly emotional language. Paul was never afraid to express his negative judgment against those who teach falsely (e.g., Gal 5:10; 1 Tim 6:3–4a). Twice he invokes his anathema uncompromisingly. The reason is not primarily to bolster his own authority but to keep in focus the divine message that he believes he has conveyed to his community faithfully. Such is the strength of Paul's message that it bore repeating.

Teaching on the Christian Faith

Saint Cyril of Jerusalem (ca. 315–ca. 386 CE), a bishop and important theologian, took inspiration from Galatians 1:9 in one of his teachings on the Christian faith:

In learning and professing the faith, you must accept and retain only the Church's present tradition, confirmed as it is by the Scriptures. Although not everyone is able to read the Scriptures, some because they have never learned to read, others because their daily activities keep them from such study, still so that their souls will not be lost through ignorance, we have gathered together the whole of the faith in a few concise articles.

Now I order you to retain this creed for your nourishment throughout life and never to accept any alternative, not even if I myself were to change and say something contrary to what I am now teaching, not even if some angel of contradiction, changed into an angel of light, tried to lead you astray. For even if we, or an angel from heaven, should preach to you a gospel contrary to that which you have now received, let him be accursed in your sight. (*De Fide et Symbolo* 12-13; PG 33, 519)

Anathema

Paul's double use of the strong Greek word *anathema* follows the usage in the LXX. The expression invokes the judgment of God on someone; it is not merely a wish for human condemnation. It is a pronouncement that one is outside the truth. Paul's usage is thus fraught with emotion and indicates just how serious he views the matter of the Galatians' desertion of his gospel (cf. 1 Cor 12:13; 16:22). The Vulgate adopts the same Greek word (*anathema*), which made its way into English primarily in ecclesiastical contexts as the equivalent of excommunication. It is no light matter to invoke such a judgment, but Paul views the situation as so critical that it is warranted.

Noteworthy in the Catholic tradition is the fact that the pope and bishops at Vatican Council II (1962-65), unlike many earlier councils convened to combat specific errors, deliberately chose not to include any anathemas in the final sixteen documents of the Council. Rather, Vatican II was a "pastoral council" seeking to reach out to the world and avoiding the strong language of condemnation.

Although Vatican II does not contain any anathemas, the Pastoral Constitution on the Church in the Modern World (*Gaudium et Spes*) strongly condemns the nuclear arms race and urges the avoidance of war (*GS* 80-81).

Paul concludes this section of his letter with two rhetorical questions and his retort, which subtly reiterates his insistence in the opening of the letter that his gospel message is not of human origin. "Am I now currying favor with human beings or God? Or am I seeking to please people?" The implied response to these two questions, in fact, is that Paul has no interest in pleasing human beings, even if he once did (perhaps in his pre-Christ life), as is hinted at by his use of the word "still" (*eti*, v. 10). His only interest is to please God.

To assert his point even more impressively, Paul employs a self-description that might, at least to modern ears, sound jarring. By paradoxically calling himself "a slave of Christ," Paul evokes a powerful image that was well known in his cultural context and that must have provoked serious reflection in his churches. Some English Bibles (NRSV, NJB, NIV) translate the Greek word *doulos* (Vulgate *servus*) as "servant." But it softens what Paul probably intends. Paul uses the expression "slave of Christ" in other instances as well (cf. Rom 1:1; Col 4:12), and it always suggests a paradoxical side to faith in Jesus Christ. In Paul's day, slaves were human property, without individual identity apart from their owners, and liable to severe treatment, although some in the Greco-Roman world were treated with a certain amount of leniency or even respect. Paul, however, asserts that he became a slave of Christ, ironically freeing him from having to worry about pleasing God by keeping the torah. For Paul, becoming a slave by the gift of faith is to become the freest individual in the world. As Paul tells the Corinthians, "For the slave called in the Lord is a freed person in the Lord, just as the free person who has been called is a slave of Christ" (1 Cor 7:22).

Ancient Greek slave working in a mine (ca. 490 BCE)

Paul's point is particularly apt in addressing the Galatians, for later in the letter, he expounds the true nature of Christian freedom (5:1–15) and why the Galatians' abandonment of his gospel message would lead them to "slavery" to the law. Contrary to a modern American understanding, freedom in Christ is not freedom *from* excessive government interference or outside constraints, but freedom to live *for* others. This slavery to Christ, then, is an act of binding oneself to the Lord in a new vein. It is a paradox. Becoming a slave of Christ ultimately leads to true freedom! Paul thus uses the title "slave of Christ" to bring the Galatians to their senses and to call them back to reexamine the nature of their faith in Christ.

PASTORAL AND SPIRITUAL OBSERVATIONS

This section of Galatians may embarrass some modern readers. Did Jesus not teach us to love our enemies (Matt 5:44), to turn the other cheek when we are mistreated (Matt 5:39), and to forgive an infinite number of times (Matt 18:21–22)? How can Paul justly react with such vehement expressions, telling the Galatians essentially that whoever is troubling them should be cast out and be damned? Paul shows his human side here by reacting in anger. Indeed, he goes so far later in the letter to wish that those demanding the Galatians be circumcised should "castrate themselves" (Gal 5:12). Paul's purpose, however, is not merely condemnatory; it is apostolic. He seeks to preserve the truth of the gospel. He wishes to bring back his beloved Galatians to that truth.

Righteous anger is hard to get right. There is always a danger of veering toward arrogant self-righteousness. That is not Paul's anger. This is not a temper tantrum. If Paul shows strong emotion here, it is because he loves the Galatians dearly and is attempting to bring them to their senses. He is like a concerned parent (Gal 4:19) who feels that his children have been led astray by deceivers who have undermined his God-given message of true freedom from the torah, and of salvation in Christ Jesus. Few of us today would be in this same position. And we must be careful not to delude ourselves into thinking our self-righteousness justifies some condemnation of others who are perceived opponents. If Paul shows righteous anger here, it is for the right reasons. He sees much at stake in the Galatians being persuaded against the gospel he had preached.

After letting off parental steam, Paul moves to a more detailed explanation of why his excited reaction to the Galatians is warranted.

REFLECTION QUESTIONS

1. Why do people write letters? Name different kinds of letters. Is Paul's letter to the Galatians a friendly one? Why or why not?
2. Paul insists on his identity as an apostle, yet he was not one of the Twelve chosen by Jesus. How does he defend this identity? Does the Lord still call "apostles" today to do his ministry? Why or why not?
3. Did Paul leave out the traditional thanksgiving section of the letter on purpose or by accident? Why? How do you think the Galatians would have reacted? How would *you* react?
4. Paul wrote letters, not a gospel. What does he mean by this all-important word *gospel*? Summarize it briefly for someone else to understand what it means.
5. What is "righteous anger"? Does the expression explain Paul's attitude in Galatians? How would you distinguish righteous anger from self-righteousness?

3

PAUL'S DEFENSE OF THE GOSPEL AND HIS AUTHORITY (1:11–2:21)

Having begun the letter and displayed some strong emotion, Paul begins a more rational presentation in showing the Galatians the error of their ways. First, he defends the gospel message he had preached, and his authority to proclaim it, by underlining his personal apostolic call from the Lord. Then, Paul recounts once more his relationship to the apostolic authorities before him, and cites agreements reached at the so-called Council of Jerusalem regarding his mission to the gentiles. He does not demur from noting the subsequent waffling on the part of Cephas and others regarding the agreements. Finally, Paul lays out the substantive theme of the letter. In contrasting the works of the law with justification by faith, Paul insists there can be no refuge in the former.

This part of the letter can be subdivided in the following five sections:

Origin of the Gospel (1:11–12)

Paul's Autobiographical Story (1:13–24)

Paul's Version of the Council of Jerusalem (2:1–10)

Paul's Confrontation of Peter at Antioch (2:11–14)

Theme of the Letter: Faith and Works (2:15–21)

ORIGIN OF THE GOSPEL (1:11-12)

[11] For I want you to know, brothers and sisters, that the gospel proclaimed by me is not of human origin; [12] neither did I receive it from a human source, nor was I taught it, but I received it through a revelation of Jesus Christ.

For 1:11, see 1 Cor 15:1

29

Paul begins his argumentation on a personal note. By addressing the Galatians as "brothers and sisters," Paul reinforces his connection with them; he does not view them as enemies, just wayward members of the community. Then with three separate expressions, Paul emphasizes the divine origin of his gospel message. It is "not of human origin," nor did he "receive it from a human being," nor was he "taught" it. This threefold denial of the human basis for the message negates both instrumentality and origin. The message Paul preached was not merely human and thus able to be compromised. No human mediated it. These denials are followed by a positive assertion: he "received it through a revelation of Jesus Christ."[1] Paul reinforces the strength of his assertion by using the first-person pronoun "I" (*egō*) in verse 12, something he does eight times in this letter;[2] its use usually indicates emphasis, strengthening Paul's claim to the divine source of his message.

This latter phrase requires comment. First, what does Paul mean by revelation? The Greek word (*apokalypsis*) refers to an unveiling or divine disclosure, from which we get the English words *apocalypse* and *apocalyptic*. It often has a connotation of dramatic events at the end time, but here it simply recalls the transcendental or nonhuman nature of Paul's experience. Paul uses the verbal form "reveal" in the next section (v. 16). Unfortunately, when we try to get behind this language to understand what he meant, we fail. All interpreters would recognize that Paul is likely referring to his "Damascus Road experience,"[3] which Acts recounts with great narrative detail and is familiar to us through many artistic portrayals. It concerns both a voice and a light, an appearance of the risen Lord Jesus who speaks to Paul (cf. Acts 9:1–9). But Paul's language is vaguer. Is he referring to a vision or an appearance of the risen Lord, as he claims elsewhere (1 Cor 15:8)? Is it perhaps a mystical experience, thus difficult to describe? He does not explain.

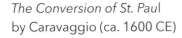

The Conversion of St. Paul
by Caravaggio (ca. 1600 CE)

He insists, though, that it was a "revelation of Jesus Christ." The preposition "of" can be troubling because here it can indicate either the origin of the revelation (*from* Jesus Christ) or the content of it (the person of the risen Lord). In this context, Paul almost certainly means that Jesus Christ was the content of this revelation. It was by means of a divine, mysterious, or perhaps a mystical revelatory experience that Paul came to know Jesus Christ, the risen Lord.

The next section (vv. 13–24) sets forth interesting details of Paul's own story, which he recalls for the Galatians because they help undergird his apostolic authority. The text can be further subdivided into two separate sections. Verses 13 to 17 recount Paul's pre-Christian life and the immediate aftermath of his commissioning as an apostle. The following section (vv. 18–24) recounts Paul's first encounter with the apostles in Jerusalem, especially those who were considered leaders of the "Jesus movement" and whose approval Paul would seek for his mission.

PAUL'S AUTOBIOGRAPHICAL STORY (1:13-24)

[13] For you have heard, no doubt, of my former life in Judaism, that I was persecuting the church of God to an extraordinary degree and, in fact, was trying to destroy it. [14] And I advanced in Judaism far beyond many of the contemporaries of my race, for I was a far more zealous adherent of the traditions handed down from my ancestors. [15] But when the One who had set me apart from my mother's womb and called me by his grace was pleased [16] to reveal his Son to me, in order that I might proclaim him to the gentiles, I did not immediately consult any human being, [17] nor did I go up to Jerusalem to those who were already apostles before me; rather I went away into Arabia, and [then] returned again to Damascus.

[18] Then after three years I went up to Jerusalem to get acquainted with Cephas and stayed with him fifteen days; [19] but I did not see any other apostle except James, the brother of the Lord. [20] (In what I am writing to you, I assure you before God, I am not lying!) [21] Then I came to the regions of Syria and Cilicia, [22] but I was still unknown by sight to the churches of Judea that are in Christ; [23] they only were hearing it said, "The one who formerly was persecuting us is now proclaiming the faith he had earlier tried to destroy." [24] And they glorified God because of me.

1:12–16: Acts 9:23–30; Acts 12:17; Rom 9:1; 2 Cor 11:31
1:15: Isa 49:1; Jer 1:4–5
1:15: Acts 7:58—8:3; 9:1–9; 26:4–5; Rom 1:5; 1 Cor 15:9–10

Having asserted the authoritative divine origin of his message, Paul now turns to what was probably a sensitive part of his personal story. He knows that the Galatians are likely aware of his background, although how many details they would have known is uncertain. He freely admits his "former way of life in Judaism," which he also recounts elsewhere in detail (cf. Phil 3:5–6). Not only that, he takes pride in this Jewish background: "advanced in Judaism far beyond many of the contemporaries of my race, for I was a far more zealous adherent of the traditions handed down from my ancestors." This is not mere family history for Paul. It helps the Galatians understand that he knows very well the value and attraction that Judaism once held for him and now holds for them. But, as he says in Philippians, all this was nothing compared to what he gained when he came to know the Lord Jesus Christ (Phil 3:8).

Paul then recalls the dramatic change that came about for him through God's intervention. Using language that evokes the call of some of the prophets in the OT, like Isaiah or Jeremiah (cf. Isa 49:1, 5–6; Jer 1:4–5), Paul describes being "set apart" and "called" for the sake of a mission; and this call has been accomplished "through his grace" (i.e., God's grace). Paul's is a prophetic call and we note that for a second time he emphasizes the content of the revelation, the person of Jesus Christ, this time using the christological title "Son." The explicit mention of Paul's mission to proclaim Christ "to the gentiles" shows just how dramatic a change came over Paul because of this divine call. Proud as he may have been, and remained, of his Jewish background, his mission was focused on converting the gentiles, which would include the Galatians. This was no mere human undertaking.

Continuing his autobiographical reminiscence and his defense of the divine nature of his call and mission, Paul then points out that he "did not immediately consult flesh and blood"—a standard biblical reference for human beings (e.g., Sir 17:31; 1 Cor 15:50); thus, Paul again denies the role of human intervention in the origin of his ministry. Paradoxically, the adverb "immediately" points to the fact that eventually, as he will narrate shortly in his letter, he did consult with human authorities in the church. Paul also denies going "up to Jerusalem" to consult with "those who were apostles before me." This is an admission on Paul's part that he knows he is hardly the first among the apostles, something that would be obvious to the Galatians. Jerusalem was the cradle of the new faith, and Paul did not hail from there. Elsewhere, Paul even notes that his apostolic call is certainly out of the ordinary, as when he includes himself in the list of those who saw the risen Lord "as one born abnormally" (1 Cor 15:8). But for Paul, while his apostleship may be out of the ordinary and his call utterly beyond human explanation, his apostleship is no less worthy than those who were before him, including the original Twelve apostles.

One might have expected Paul to feel insecure as an apostle, since he was not a companion of the earthly Jesus. Thus, one might also have expected him to seek legitimation by consulting with prior authorities. In contrast, Paul says obscurely, "Rather, I went away into Arabia and [then] returned again to Damascus." The return to Damascus is perhaps easily explained because that was the approximate location of his call, his revelation of Jesus Christ. According to Acts, that is where Paul was baptized and immediately began his mission (cf. Acts 9:18–20). But the mention of Arabia is more puzzling. Geographically, what is meant is not modern Saudi Arabia, but ancient Nabatea, an area southeast of Damascus and the Holy Land, a desert area where early Christians had settled. Paul does not explain why he went there. Was it to flee the scene after his call? After all, his reputation as a persecutor frightened many Christians who may have thought his conversion phony. Or was it to connect with early Christians and be tutored somewhat in the new faith? Though Paul shows some awareness of the traditions about Jesus of Nazareth, he seemingly has little interest in them. Yet somehow Paul did encounter an already existent Christian tradition. Or did he go to Nabatea perhaps because, like Elijah the prophet before him, he went into the desert to encounter God and to prepare for battle with the forces of evil (cf. 1 Kgs 19:1–18)?[4]

Why Arabia?

The matter of identifying the location of Paul's sojourn in "Arabia" (2:17) is not as easy as it might seem. The Hebrew OT does not record a place called "Arabia," referring rather to Arabians as the people from "the land of the East" (Gen 25:6; 29:1; Judg 6:3; Isa 11:14), including ancient kingdoms like Midian, Moab, and Edom. Over time, Arabia became associated with the desert, an arid wilderness.

In the NT, "Arabs" are included in the list of foreigners gathered in Jerusalem on the day of Pentecost (Acts 2:11). Paul specifies neither the precise region nor the duration of his stay in "Arabia." Most scholars today identify the region with Nabatea, a kingdom to the southeast of Damascus. This proposal is reasonable for three reasons. First, its relative proximity to Damascus makes sense and would have enabled Paul to get off the scene shortly after his conversion because of his notoriety as an extreme persecutor of the church (Acts 9:23–25). Second, the region was a site of early Christian preachers, which may have brought Paul into contact with some believers who preceded him in the faith. Finally, the region was a desert area, which may have afforded Paul time to spend in prayer and preparation for his later missionary journeys.

Map of First-century Palestine and Nabatea

Paul admits that he did go to Jerusalem for a short visit, but only "after three years" and only spending a short time of "fifteen days" (two weeks, in biblical parlance) with "Cephas (=Kephas)" and "James the brother of the Lord." Kephas, meaning "rock,"[5] was Peter's Aramaic name, so clearly, Paul acknowledges having consulted Peter, the chief spokesman of the original Twelve apostles and the head of the Christians gathered in Jerusalem, and consulting James, who later became Peter's successor at the head of the Jerusalem church and was martyred in 62 CE. Although the brevity of the visit shows it was not an official meeting, it nevertheless demonstrates Paul's willingness to work with authorities in the Church who preceded his own apostolic call. He is not a loner in ministry, but note that he may suspect some will doubt his word, for he immediately adds a side comment (indicated by parentheses) that "I assure you, before God, I am not lying." He forestalls any objection the Galatians might make by invoking his truthfulness.

After this brief visit, Paul says he went to "the regions of Syria and Cilicia." This is an early part of Paul's ministry of evangelization about which we have very little information, whether from Acts (15:41) or his own letters. Going back to Damascus may have been risky because of his reputation as a persecutor, but going to Cilicia, his native territory in the mountains of Asia Minor, took him back home from where he could launch other missionary forays into central Asia Minor, home of the ethnic Galatians, as well as elsewhere. Paul humbly admits that at this point in his apostolic mission he is not well-known, especially "to the churches of Judea that are in Christ."[6] Judea represents the southern region of the Holy Land, in contrast to Israel in the north, and it could be considered the cradle of early Christianity because of the beginnings of the faith in Jerusalem and surrounding area. Paul even acknowledges that his notoriety as a now-converted persecutor had preceded him: "They only kept hearing that 'the one who formerly was persecuting us is now proclaiming the faith he had earlier tried to destroy.'" This may have been a startling message for these faithful, but Paul says the reaction was nothing but positive, for in the end, "they glorified God because of me [or 'on my account']." This is like receiving the *Good Housekeeping* Seal of Approval. Paul was considered by the founding communities to have become an authentic proclaimer of the faith. This helps reinforce Paul's authority and the outreach of his ministry to the gentiles. It also helps bolster Paul's arguments later in the letter to call the Galatians back to the faith he had preached to them, for his call was neither a fluke nor a fraud.

James the Brother of the Lord

The NT mentions several men with the common name James. The precise nature of this James the brother of the Lord's relationship to Jesus is not known. He was clearly a relative (cf. 1 Cor 9:5; Acts 12:17; 15:13–21) but not a member of the Twelve, though he was an apostle (1 Cor 15:7). The Greek word *adelphos* has a wider meaning than simply blood brother; it can mean a cousin or other relation. Since patristic times, interpreters have debated how best to understand this designation. Some fathers of the Church, like Epiphanius, thought he was the son of Joseph by a previous marriage, thus Jesus's stepbrother. Ambrosiaster, Jerome, Augustine, and others thought he might have been a relative of Jesus by Mary's family. Augustine explicitly says, "James is understood to be the Lord's brother because he was one of Joseph's sons by another wife or perhaps one of the relatives of the Lord's mother Mary" (Plumer, 135).

While Protestants have tended to accept the literalness of the expression "brother of the Lord," the Catholic Church has taught that it does not mean that, because of the doctrine of the perpetual virginity of the Blessed Virgin Mary. In Catholic teaching, Mary and Joseph had no other children, and Mary miraculously guarded her virginity, despite having given birth to Jesus. Catholic translations, including the lectionary, rightly maintain the literal expression "James the brother of the Lord."

Most scholars judge unlikely the possibility that this James is the (unknown) author of the Letter of James in the NT. Nothing in the letter associates it with a relative of Jesus.

Possible Contact between Paul's Letters and the Gospel Traditions		
REFERENCES	PAUL'S WORDS	GOSPEL ALLUSION
1 Thess 5:2 // Matt 24:42-43	"For you yourselves know very well that the day of the Lord will come like a thief in the night."	"Keep awake therefore, for you do not know on what day your Lord is coming. But understand this: if the owner of the house had known in what part of the night the thief was coming, he would have stayed awake and would not have let his house be broken into."
1 Cor 10:27 // Luke 10:8	"If an unbeliever invites you to a meal and you are disposed to go, eat whatever is set before you without raising any question on the ground of conscience."	"Whenever you enter a town and its people welcome you, eat what is set before you."
Rom 12:14 // Matt 5:44	"Bless those who persecute you; bless and do not curse them."	"But I say to you, Love your enemies and pray for those who persecute you."

Continued

Rom 13:8-10 // Matt 22:39-40	"Owe no one anything, except to love one another; for the one who loves another has fulfilled the law. The commandments…are summed up in this word, 'Love your neighbor as yourself.' Love does no wrong to a neighbor; therefore, love is the fulfilling of the law."	"And a second is like it: 'You shall love your neighbor as yourself.' On these two commandments hang all the law and the prophets."
Rom 14:13 // Matt 7:1	"Let us therefore no longer pass judgment on one another, but resolve instead never to put a stumbling block or hindrance in the way of another."	"Do not judge, so that you may not be judged."
1 Cor 4:2 // Luke 12:42	"Moreover, it is required of stewards that they be found trustworthy."	"Who then is the faithful and wise steward, whom his master will set over his household?" (au. trans.)
Rom 16:19 // Matt 10:16	"I would have you wise as to what is good and guileless as to what is evil." (au. trans.)	"So be wise as serpents and innocent as doves."
Rom 14:14 // Mark 7:15	"I know and am persuaded that nothing is unclean in itself."	"There is nothing outside a man that by going in can defile him."
1 Cor 15:50 // John 3:5-6	"Flesh and blood cannot inherit the kingdom of God."	"Truly, truly, I say to you, unless one is born of water and the Spirit, he cannot enter the kingdom of God. That which is born of the flesh is flesh, and that which is born of the Spirit is spirit." (au. trans.)
Rom 14:17 // Matt 6:33	"For the kingdom of God is not food and drink but righteousness and peace and joy in the Holy Spirit."	"But seek first his [God's] kingdom and his righteousness, and all these things shall be yours as well." (au. trans.)

Continued

GALATIANS

1 Cor 4:20 // Mark 9:1	"For the kingdom of God does not consist in talk but in power." (au. trans.)	"Truly, I say to you, there are some standing here who will not taste death before they see the kingdom of God has come with power." (au. trans.)
1 Cor 7:10 // Mark 10:11; see Matt 5:32; Luke 19:9	"The wife should not separate from her husband."	"Whoever divorces his wife and marries another commits adultery against her."
1 Cor 11:24 // Luke 22:19; see Mark 14:22; Matt 26:26	"This is my body that is for you. Do this in remembrance of me."	"This is my body, which is given for you. Do this in remembrance of me."

As a further expansion of his autobiographical data, Paul recounts his view of the Council of Jerusalem and its aftermath, which gave impetus to his mission to gentiles. The passage accomplishes two tasks simultaneously. On the one hand, it bolsters Paul's authority to proclaim his gospel message; on the other hand, it lays the groundwork for Paul to call back sharply the Galatians from submitting to the agitators' summons to Jewish practices that no longer serve salvation.

PAUL'S VERSION OF THE COUNCIL OF JERUSALEM (2:1–10)

2 ¹ Then after fourteen years I went up again to Jerusalem with Barnabas, taking Titus along also. ² I went up because of a revelation, and I laid out to them (though only in a private meeting with the acknowledged leaders) the gospel that I preach among the gentiles, lest somehow I was running, or had run, in vain. ³ But not even Titus, who was with me, although he was a Greek, was compelled to be circumcised.

⁴ Now because of certain false brothers secretly brought in, who slipped in to spy on our freedom that we have in Christ Jesus, so that they might enslave us— ⁵ we did not submit to them even for a moment, so that the truth of the gospel might always remain intact with you. ⁶ But from those who were reputed leaders (what they actually were makes no difference to me; God shows no partiality)— for those leaders contributed nothing to me. ⁷ On the contrary, when they saw that I had been entrusted with the gospel for the uncircumcised, just as Peter had been entrusted the same for the circumcised ⁸ (for the one who was at work through Peter, making him an apostle to the circumcised, also worked through

me for the gentiles), ⁹ and when James and Cephas and John, who were reputed pillars, recognized the grace that had been given to me, they gave to me and Barnabas the right hand of fellowship, in order that we should go to the gentiles and they to the circumcision. ¹⁰ They asked only one thing, namely, that we remember the poor, the very thing I was also eager to do.

2:6: Deut 10:17; NT: Rom 2:11
2:7–10: Acts 11:29–30; 15:1–21, 25–28; 1 Cor 16:1–4;
2 Cor 8:1–15

Paul tells of another visit to Jerusalem with his colleagues, Barnabas, who had in fact enlisted Paul in ministry and was his mentor (Acts 9:27), and Titus, a younger colleague in whom Paul had much confidence (2 Cor 7:13b–14). Placing this visit in the context of Paul's apostolic career has always been a challenge because of the expression "fourteen years." Does it refer to the time since his conversion? After the first trip to Jerusalem? He does not specify, but obviously, Paul had already been actively evangelizing for a considerable time and had accumulated extensive experience. More importantly, he underlines that he went to Jerusalem "because of a revelation" (NRSV "in response to a revelation"). This means God is once more intervening directly in Paul's ministry, and it bolsters his authority, even as he goes to meet the well-known authorities of the mother church, the "acknowledged leaders." Paul twice mentions those of repute (vv. 2 and 9), going on to call at least some of them whom he will name "pillars." Along with these acknowledgments of the genuine authority of the early apostolic leaders, who function like the pillars or the firm apostolic foundation upon which Jesus erected his church (cf. Matt 16:18), Paul is also quite explicit that he presented to these same authorities, who will be named shortly, "the gospel that I preach among the gentiles." In other words, he lays out his customary message, as if for examination and approval, but "privately," probably to avoid any possible embarrassment for himself or the authorities, should questions arise.

Paul and His Colleagues

BARNABAS

Barnabas, a Levite and native of Cyprus, figures prominently in Galatians (2:1-13). Acts also mentions him numerous times and says that his name was changed from Joseph to Barnabas, "son of encouragement," perhaps because of his generosity in selling some property and donating the proceeds to the church (Acts 4:36-37).

Barnabas was a prominent figure in the Jerusalem church, and then later in Antioch, where he was known as one of the "prophets and teachers" (Acts 13:1). Acts recounts his connection to Paul (9:27; 11:25-30). After the latter's conversion, he sought out the new convert to bring him to the apostles in Jerusalem (9:27) who were impressed enough to send both together on mission to Antioch in Syria. Barnabas is also called an "apostle" along with Paul (14:14), the only place in Acts where the title is accorded to Paul apart from the Twelve.

Originally, Paul was the understudy of Barnabas, as is apparent from the fact that Barnabas is usually named first. But at some point that situation changed, evident in the reversal of the order of the names (Acts 13:43). Also, at Iconium, Paul is featured as the primary spokesman in the missionary team: "They called Barnabas 'Zeus' and Paul 'Hermes,' because he was the chief speaker" (14:12).

Acts 15:36-40 also narrates that Paul and Barnabas had a big falling out over a controversy involving a certain John Mark whom Paul did not trust but whom Barnabas wanted as a companion. Acts explains, "So sharp was their disagreement that they separated" (15:39). John Mark was probably a relative of Barnabas, for Colossians refers to a "Mark the cousin of Barnabas" (Col 4:10). The result was that Barnabas went his own way with Mark, and Paul chose Silas to go another direction (Acts 15:39-40). Even in the early church cooperative ministry was a struggle!

TITUS

Unlike some of Paul's other famous companions, Titus is never mentioned in Acts. We know of him only from Paul's letters. The Letter to Titus testifies to his status as a trusted younger colleague of Paul.

Titus was a gentile Christian whom Paul calls "my partner and co-worker" (2 Cor 8:23). His main service to Paul was serving as a courier to the Corinthian community, with whom he had a strong relationship (2 Cor 7:13-14). He also helped Paul collect money from the Corinthians for the support of the Jerusalem church (2 Cor 8:1-7).

Titus is mentioned in Galatians because he serves as concrete evidence, a type of test case, that one need not be circumcised, that is, become a Jew, in order to follow Christ (Gal 2:1-3). The fact that he was not compelled to be circumcised, despite his Greek heritage, spoke forcefully "in the flesh" for Paul, and was meant to recall for the Galatians Paul's message that the law did not apply to non-Jews.

Jew and Gentile: What Was at Stake?

Modern readers of the NT may have some difficulty understanding just what was at stake in the difference between Jewish and gentile identity that forms the backdrop of Galatians. Separation was the norm. Jews distinguished themselves strongly from the "nations." They based their identity on the covenant with God, the God of the patriarchs—Abraham, Isaac, and Jacob—and they understood in this divine election that God had bestowed upon them a special, unique identity. In the Book of Exodus, God says to Moses,

> Now therefore, if you obey my voice and keep my covenant, you shall be my treasured possession out of all the peoples. Indeed, the whole earth is mine, but you shall be for me a priestly kingdom and a holy nation. (Exod 19:5-6; also, Deut 14:2 NRSV)

Furthermore, Deuteronomy explains that the sole reason God chose Israel for this special identity was out of love and faithfulness to the covenant:

> It was not because you were more numerous than any other people that the LORD set his heart on you and chose you—for you were the fewest of all peoples. It was because the LORD loved you and kept the oath that he swore to your ancestors, that the LORD has brought you out with a mighty hand, and redeemed you from the house of slavery, from the hand of Pharaoh king of Egypt. (Deut 7:7-8 NRSV)

This identity, then, was rooted in love, election, and covenant. God "redeemed" Israel from slavery. God favored them, agreeing to become their God, and they to be God's people. With this agreement, however, came obligations to observe the commandments of the law strictly, not just circumcision, but especially the dietary laws and those tied to the issues of purity. Maintaining ritual purity was crucial because Israel was called to be holy (Heb. *qadosh*), which means "set apart." They were not to be like the other nations (Heb. *goiim*; Gk. *ethnē*, "gentiles"). They were to be holy as God alone is holy (cf. Lev 11:44).

A text from late Judaism, about 140 years before Jesus, illustrates the point. The Book of Jubilees, an apocryphal work from the second century BCE, shows just how strong the separation between the Jews and gentiles may have been:

> Remember my words, Jacob my son, and observe the commandments of Abraham, your father: Separate yourself from the nations and do not eat with them; and do not act according to their works, and do not

associate with them; for their works are unclean, and all their ways are a pollution and an abomination and impurity. (Jub 22:16)

The great Jewish prayer prayed by pious Jews every day, the *Shema' Yisrael* ("Hear, O Israel"), reminded the Jews of the obligation to observe God's commands and thereby preserve their unique identity. Over time, these obligations became expanded, more codified, and precise. With the experience of the exile and being dispersed all over the known world, the question of identity became even more critical. By the time of Alexander the Great and his successors (fourth century BCE), and under the influence of the Roman Empire, the pressures on Jews from the dominant culture became more intense. To maintain purity, they had to restrict contact with gentiles, especially meals, refrain from buying meat in the market for fear it may have been involved in pagan sacrificial rituals, and so on. Jews also developed practices to remember the law. Jewish males took literally to binding quotations from the law to their foreheads and wrists (called "phylacteries"; see Deut 6:8-9), and Jewish houses bore a small excerpt of the law in a container at their entrance (called the "mezuzah").

Gentiles often viewed such practices as quaint or superstitious, but for Jews, these were marks of identity rooted in the obligations of the Mosaic law. Importantly, Paul, himself a Pharisaic Jew (Phil 3:5), knew the value of these practices *for Jews*. But he also realized that, in Christ, they held no obligation *for gentiles*. His gospel message was freedom from such obligations. Being in Christ bestowed a different kind of identity (new creation!, 6:15), with a different kind of marking (baptism and the cross). Moreover, given the strong urge toward separation between Jews and gentiles, Paul's forceful message of unity and the lack of distinctions among humans (3:28) made a strong impact. So, what is at stake in Paul's argument is nothing less than reminding the Galatians that neither dietary restrictions (2:12) nor circumcision (5:2-3) bestowed upon them their true identity in Christ.

Council of Jerusalem: Tensions between Galatians and Acts		
Category	**Gal 2:1-14**	**Acts 15:1-10, 11-31**
Date	"Fourteen years" after his first visit to Jerusalem; that is, during Paul's second visit (v. 1)	During Paul's third or fourth visit to Jerusalem (see 12:25; 9:26-30; 11:29-30 for earlier visits) after preaching in Antioch.

Continued

Paul's Defense of the Gospel and His Authority (1:11—2:21)   41

Principal Actors	Paul is the primary figure, with Barnabas and Titus; Peter and James are portrayed as honored leaders but obstacles to some degree.	Peter and James are the primary figures; Paul and Barnabas and "some others" go to Jerusalem.
Motivation and Outcome	Paul goes to Jerusalem in accordance with a "revelation" to meet with the reputed "pillars" of the church to confirm his "gospel to the gentiles" (vv. 1–2, 9).	Because of a debate about circumcision for the gentiles, Paul and Barnabas are sent to Jerusalem to consult the apostles and presbyters about the matter (vv. 1–2).
	Paul reports "privately to those of repute."	The whole Jerusalem church welcomes them and hears their report.
	Titus is not compelled to be circumcised (v. 3).	(Paul has another colleague, Timothy, whose father was Greek, circumcised "on account of the Jews" [Acts 16:3]).
	Some "false brothers" slipped in to try to sabotage Paul's efforts (v. 4).	
	James, Cephas, and John confirm Paul's ministry to the gentiles, as well as Peter's (Cephas) to the Jews (vv. 7–8).	After much debate, Peter spoke to those assembled and confirmed Paul's ministry to the gentiles and that "Jewish" burdens should not be placed upon them (vv. 6–11).
	Paul agrees to take up a collection for the poor in Jerusalem (v. 10).	(Acts 11:30 infers a collection)
Problem	Later, Cephas came to Antioch and, under the influence of followers of James, leader of the Jerusalem church, he and Barnabas stopped eating with the gentiles; Paul is incensed at their hypocrisy and opposes Cephas publicly (vv. 11–14).	James, leader of the Jerusalem church, spoke to the assembly and confirms that they should not "trouble the gentiles" but only insist that they refrain from idolatry, fornication, unclean food, and blood; they send a letter with Paul, Barnabas, and the others outlining this decision (vv. 13–29).
		The community in Antioch is delighted (v. 31)

Continued

GALATIANS

	Circumcision and eating unclean foods.	Idolatry, fornication, eating unclean foods, and blood, although circumcision was the original issue (v. 1).
Underlying Controversy		
Resolution	Paul is forced to defend his special mission to the gentiles by confronting Peter's compromise of abstaining from table fellowship with gentiles in the face of opposition from those associated with James who were promoting observance of the Mosaic law.	Peter and James both confirm Paul's mission to the gentiles.

The reason Paul gives for this consultation is "lest somehow I was running, or had run, in vain." Here, Paul uses one of his sports metaphors that appear periodically in his letters (1 Cor 9:24–26; Phil 4:1). It is the image of a race he does not want to have run in vain (see the similar expression in Phil 2:16). But to what does this refer? He is not concerned about the truth of his gospel message, which he has already asserted several times in the letter, nor is he preoccupied with the blessing he knows he received from the proper church authorities, which he will recount for the Galatians. His concern, rather, is that he wanted to ensure that his ministry to the gentiles would have its ultimate effect, namely, that they would reach the finish line of salvation on an equal footing with the Jewish Christians. As he writes of the gentiles eloquently in Ephesians,

> So then you are no longer strangers and aliens, but you are citizens with the saints and also members of the household of God, built upon the foundation of the apostles and prophets, with Christ Jesus himself as the cornerstone. (Eph 2:19–20 NRSV)

In a sense, Paul views his ministry like a race in which one must put forth the best possible effort to achieve the desired goal.

Paul and Athletics

Paul might well be considered the first Christian sports fan. (Many more have followed!) He regularly uses athletic imagery in his letters to illustrate his message. He thus shows familiarity with one of the common features of the

Greco-Roman world in which he lived. As a Jew living in a major city in the diaspora, Paul would have been familiar with the gymnasium, the place where boys and men went to exercise and hone their athletic skills.

Athletics were a common feature in the Greco-Roman world. The word derives from a Greek word (*athleō*) meaning to "contend for a prize." In Paul's world, sports were diverse and included running, jumping, sprinting, boxing, wrestling, discus, and javelin throwing. Athletics were not merely a matter of competition, fostered in well-known games such as the Olympics—likely the most renowned of the games—the Isthmian games (held near Corinth), the Pythian games, or the Nemean games, all held at diverse locations in Greece at periods of between two and four years. In addition, athletics were also part of the system of education of boys to become adult citizens of a city. The primary center for athletics was consequently the gymnasium, a building built around an athletic field, where boys not only exercised their bodies but would also learn other useful subjects, such as liberal arts and music, to exercise their minds.

Since the time of the Maccabeans, some Jews had resisted participating in athletics because of their association with pagan rituals (see 2 Macc 4:12–20). Particularly offensive for Jews was the Greek practice of exercising in the gymnasium in the nude (from Gk. *gymnos*, "naked"), which made it easy to distinguish one's religious identity (see 1 Macc 1:13–15), since Jews were circumcised. Jews in Palestine resisted such Hellenistic institutions, as is attested in the writings of the Jewish-Roman historian Josephus (*Antiquities* 15.8.1 §268). Archaeology, however, has shown that there were gymnasia and other Greco-Roman buildings even in Galilee, not far from Nazareth, at a village called Sepphoris! Over time, Jewish males in the diaspora adapted more readily to local customs and often participated freely in athletics, as can be seen from the Jewish philosopher Philo of Alexandria (*Omn. Prob. Lib.* 26) and the Books of Maccabees (referenced above).

Athletics also provided many metaphors for philosophers in the ancient world, especially Stoics and Cynics. The image of discipline and the physical and mental training required to be a successful athlete lent itself well to speaking about such practices for promoting a virtuous life. The NT also attests to familiarity with this metaphorical use of athletic imagery, especially in the letters of Paul (Rom 9:16; 13:12; 1 Cor 9:24–27; Phil 2:16; Gal 2:2; 5:7; 1 Thess 2:4; see also Luke 22:44). A healthy spirituality, like athletics, requires discipline and practice.

Two Greco-Roman athletes wrestling

Paul then offers the Galatians an example of the generosity of the authorities in approving of his outreach to the gentiles. He says that "not even Titus, who was with me, although he was a Greek, was compelled to be circumcised." Paul uses Titus here as "exhibit A" in defense of his consistent message that one does not need to be circumcised to be a follower of Jesus Christ. Paul will speak of this issue at greater length in the letter, but the mention of Titus here is enough evidence to make his point. Even the pillars of the church did not require this gentile to be circumcised.

But that was not the end of the story. For Paul, using language that hints at major themes to come (freedom, slavery), speaks of certain "unnamed false brothers secretly brought in, who slipped in to spy on our freedom that we have in Christ Jesus, so that they might enslave us." Paul minces no words in calling these opponents "false brothers" (*pseudalphous*). They represent a coercive attempt to combat the freedom from the law that comes with life in Jesus Christ. Paul likens them to spies who secretly try to undermine the truth. They "slipped in," he says, but his assertion that they were "brought in" implies collusion on the part of some person(s) inside the community. At this point in the church's history, unanimity was hardly a given, and Paul alleges that the subtle attempt to undermine his mission perhaps came from within. He insists, however, that "we did not submit even for a moment, so that the truth of the gospel might remain intact for you." The phrase "even of a moment" (lit. "even for an hour") indicates the haste with which Paul and his colleagues reacted to the agitators, a subtle retort to the haste with which the Galatians have abandoned the gospel (1:6). Here, Paul champions his resistance to the attempt to undermine his gentile mission for the express reason to safeguard "the truth of the gospel" (see also v. 14). This expression constitutes an underlying leitmotif in Galatians. Eternal truth, rooted in the gospel of Jesus Christ, is exactly what is at stake for Paul. The gospel should not be perverted (1:7). His unwavering resistance to any corruption of his approach is so that his churches in Galatia could remain free.

Then Paul again appeals to "those who were reputed leaders," though he quickly says in an aside that it is not their status that is so crucial but their actions. In terms of status before God, Paul states explicitly that "God shows no partiality" (see also Rom 2:11; Eph 6:9). What was critical for Paul is that these authorities "contributed nothing to me," meaning that they did not impose other requirements or restrictions. Paul implies that they accepted his basic missionary approach without modification.

Circumcision

The origins of the practice of circumcision are lost in time. The practice may have arisen in ancient Egypt for hygienic reasons, though this is uncertain. In any case, it was a prominent custom in the ancient Near East among Semitic peoples. The Jews, however, developed a particularly rich and complex meaning for the practice. Circumcision of male infants on the eighth day after their birth was a religious ritual. In Jewish theology it originated with the covenant God offered to Abraham (Gen 17:9-14; see also Josh 5:2-9). Circumcision was a physical sign of belonging to the Jewish people, God's chosen ones (Lev 12:3). It served as a virtual identification badge. It marked an individual as a sacred person belonging to God's special people. To disregard circumcision was tantamount to self-excommunication from the people of God.

The practice became a critical identity marker for Jews especially during the time of the Maccabeans (second century BCE), when Hellenistic culture dominated Palestine and the entire Greco-Roman world. Some Jews, especially in the diaspora, attempted to hide or reverse their circumcision (1 Macc 1:14–15) in order to be more welcomed in such a secular environment. Law-observant Jews considered this practice a vile act of betrayal of one's very identity as a Jew and a desecration of God's covenant with Abraham.

In such a context, Paul's teaching that circumcision was no longer a necessary requirement for a gentile to become a follower of Jesus would have been a radical and abhorrent idea for many Jewish Christians. The agitators in Galatia apparently persuaded the Galatians to adopt the practice of circumcision, contrary to what Paul preached.

We do not know exactly where or when Paul came to the realization that circumcision—that is, becoming a Jew—was no longer needed once one was baptized into Christ Jesus. But this was an essential part of his gospel message and was approved by the Jerusalem leaders. Thus he is incredibly upset when Peter, and even Barnabas, renege, and he learns that certain people from James are undermining his teaching.

If Paul put no stock in the physical act of circumcision, he nonetheless understood it metaphorically, a concept also found in the OT with phrases such as "circumcise the foreskins of your heart" (Deut 10:16; cf. 30:6; Lev 26:41; Jer 4:4); or having "uncircumcised ears" (Jer 6:10). In Romans, Paul says, "One is not a Jew outwardly. True circumcision is not outward, in the flesh. Rather, one is a Jew inwardly, and circumcision is of the heart, in the spirit, not the letter" (2:28–29 NABRE).

Unlike the OT, where even the aliens among the Israelites were required to be circumcised (Exod 12:48), the physical act of circumcision was irrelevant for those in Christ. Paul was not against circumcision of Jews (or anyone who wanted to accept it). But he opposed it as obligatory for gentiles to enter the family of faith in Christ. It was unnecessary and brought no benefit (Gal 5:2). One's new baptismal identity came with Christ, not by circumcision. Neither circumcision nor uncircumcision mattered (Gal 6:15).

The next three verses (vv. 7–9) compare and contrast Paul's mission to the "uncircumcised" (gentiles) to Peter's mission to the "circumcised" (Jews). Using the concept at the very heart of the controversy, circumcision, Paul points out that his mission was confirmed by those "reputed pillars," naming again James and Cephas, but this time adding John, who is certainly one of the Twelve (probably one of Zebedee's sons, cf. Mark 1:19) and a noted leader in the Jerusalem church as well.[7]

Paul offers two explanations for their support. The first reason is the recognition that the same God was at work in the mission to the Jews and the gentiles. In Paul's words, "For the one who was at work through Peter, making him an apostle to the circumcised, also worked through me for the gentiles." This dual mission of the church has only one source, God. The second reason is that "they recognized the grace bestowed upon me." Paul does not specify who "they" were, but this probably refers to a wider circle of significant leaders in Jerusalem, among whom the inner circle of power figures also operated. The reference to "grace" serves as a strong reminder that God had ordained Paul's mission. His call is due to God's grace at work in him (1:15), and that same grace of God had called the Galatians to faith (1:6). The authorities, then, recognized God's grace at work in Paul's ministry. Paul confirms even that the pillars "gave me and Barnabas the right hand of fellowship."[8] They shook hands on it, making it an understood agreement, with the result that "we should go to the gentiles and they to the circumcised." The validity of a bidirectional evangelical outreach to gentile and Jew alike was thus preserved by this agreement.

Right Hand versus Left Hand

It is statistically verifiable that most people are right-handed rather than left. But does this matter in the biblical worldview? If you are left-handed, I am sorry to say, you will be disappointed.

The Bible, in fact, mentions the expression "right hand" dozens of time, both about God and human beings. Except for contexts wherein right and left are being contrasted, left-handedness is rarely mentioned, only about a dozen times. Actions with the left hand are less honorable. Offering someone the "right hand of fellowship" is an honorable deed and is presumed to be trustworthy.

In the OT, God acts with his "right hand (or arm)" (Exod 15:6; Pss 18:35; 44:3; 45:4) and so do God's agents (Judg 5:26; 2 Sam 20:9). Blessings are given with the right hand (Gen 48:13–18), and the preferred place in God's kingdom is always on the right (Pss 16:8; 17:7). The NT most often speaks of the right hand of God as the place where the risen and glorified Christ sits (Rom 8:34; Eph 1:20; Col 3:1; Heb 1:3, 13; 8:1; 10:12; 1 Pet 3:22; etc.).

In short, regardless of the reason(s), right-handedness is associated with the norm of honorable divine and human behavior.

Paul concludes this section with a terse notice that the authorities in Jerusalem had asked only one favor of Paul and his colleagues: "remember the poor." Paul quickly adds that not only was this acceptable, but he was anxious to fulfill this request, "the very thing I was also eager to do." Although Paul certainly was mindful of the poor in general (2 Cor 9:9, citing Ps 112:9), a duty typical of Judaism (Lev 19:10; Isa 10:1–2; Prov 14:21) and also characteristic of the teaching of Jesus (Matt 19:21; Mark 10:21; Luke 4:18; 14:13, 21), the poor in this context means the poor of Jerusalem, the mother church. This line, then, spoken noticeably in first person to underline Paul's personal commitment, refers to the collection among his wealthier gentile churches in the diaspora that Paul undertook to support the "poor among the saints at Jerusalem" (Rom 15:26; on the collection, see especially 2 Cor 8:1—9:15). This expectation was to preoccupy Paul for some twenty years of his ministry. He even desired to ensure that it was delivered personally to fulfill this one demand (Rom 15:28).

Icon of the apostles Sts. Peter and Paul

Turning from the results of the Council of Jerusalem, Paul recounts an incident in Antioch that drew his ire. He narrates another incidence of certain forces from within the church in Jerusalem that attempted to undermine table fellowship with the gentiles that Paul had thought already decided.

PAUL'S CONFRONTATION OF PETER AT ANTIOCH (2:11–14)

[11] But when Cephas came to Antioch, I opposed him to his face, because he stood self-condemned; [12] for until certain people came from James, he used to eat with the gentiles. But after they came, he withdrew and kept himself separate for fear of the circumcision faction, [13] and the rest of the Jews also joined him in this hypocrisy, so that even Barnabas was carried away with them in their hypocrisy. [14] But when I saw that they were not being straightforward with the truth of the gospel, I said to Cephas before them all, "If you, though a Jew, live like a gentile and not like a Jew, how can you compel the gentiles to live like Jews?"

2:11: Acts 11:19–30; 15:1–2
2:12: Acts 10:15, 28; 11:3
2:14: Rom 3:20, 28; Eph 2:8–9

Cephas is again at the center of the controversy Paul raises. Sometime after the Council of Jerusalem, Cephas came to Antioch and, Paul claims, in essence, "I opposed him to his face because he clearly was wrong." Paul shows no hesitancy to make this judgment, so convinced is he of the truth of his position. The reason for his confidence becomes clear in the next three verses (vv. 12–14). A group of agitators came to Antioch to stir up trouble, precisely because of the dietary regulations of the Mosaic law. Paul now identifies them as "certain people" who "came from James." Paul claims that Peter (Cephas) "used to eat with the gentiles" until this Jerusalem delegation arrived, but after their arrival "he withdrew and kept himself separate for fear of the circumcision faction." In other words, Cephas's actions provide the condemnation. The form of the verb "used to eat" (*synēsthien*), as the translation indicates, points to habitual behavior. In other words, Peter, despite his own Jewish background and his leadership position, had become accustomed to table fellowship with gentiles, the uncircumcised, with whom Jews normally preferred to refrain from close contact. Paul is obviously incensed that Peter caves in to the pressure from James's people out of fear. Social pressures can be hard to resist, as Paul indicates when he says that "the rest of the Jews also joined him in this hypocrisy." Even more galling for Paul is the fact that his mentor and colleague fell for the same unacceptable action: "even Barnabas was carried away with them in their hypocrisy." The verb "carried away" (NRSV, NET, NIV "led astray") may soften somewhat Barnabas's betrayal in that he was misled by others, but the adverb "even" betrays Paul's disappointment with his colleague. By labeling this action "hypocrisy," Paul associates it with the worst type of duplicity.

Interpretations of Paul's Confrontation with Peter

John Calvin (1509-64), the great Protestant Reformer, sees more importance to the action of Paul confronting Peter directly (Gal 2:11) than some interpreters might suggest. He sees it as a courageous act in which Paul saw what was really at stake. Then Calvin applies it to our own situation. He observes,

> If Paul had been silent here, his whole doctrine fell; all the edification obtained by his ministry was ruined. It was therefore necessary that he should rise manfully, and fight with courage. This shows us how cautiously we ought to guard against giving away to the opinions of human beings, lest an immoderate desire to please, or an undue dread of giving offence, should turn us aside from the right path. If this might happen to Peter, how much more easily may it happen to us, if we are not duly careful! (Calvin, 63)

In his commentary on Galatians, Marius Victorinus (ca. 283-362), who wrote the earliest Latin commentaries on Paul's letters in existence, uses the serious term "sin" (Lat. *peccatum*) for Peter's waffling on the issue of table fellowship with gentiles out of fear of the Jewish party. While he sees this action as "a small thing," he nevertheless considers it seriously sinful because it influenced others to cave in as well, including Barnabas. This enhanced Cephas's guilt (Cooper, 278-79). Saint Augustine, on the other hand, who also admits that Cephas "feared" those who came from Jerusalem, prefers to use the term "error" (Lat. *error*), perhaps softening somewhat Cephas's mistake (Plumer, 145).

While there are nuances in interpretation, these three cases indicate that much was indeed at stake and that Paul was justified in confronting the spokesman of the apostles.

The root idea of hypocrisy is wearing a mask; the concept came out of the world of Greek theater, where actors would use masks to portray one or another characteristic. Moral hypocrisy is when one's words or demeanor say one thing, while one's actions betray another. It is not being genuine. Paul sees it as equivalent to compromising "the truth of the gospel" (2:5, 14). In another context, Jesus rails against the hypocrisy of some of the Jewish leadership (Matt 7:5; 15:7; 23:13, 15, 25, 27, 29; Luke 12:56; 13:15). Interestingly, Paul says simply that "they were not being straightforward with the truth of the gospel." His own road to conversion had been a twisted one that ultimately led to "the street called Straight" (Acts 9:11). Here he sees others detouring from the sure path of the truth. At stake again was a truth for which Paul will not and cannot compromise, because it is God's truth.

In contrast to the private consultation mentioned earlier (2:3), Paul claims that he confronted Peter directly and publicly: "I said to Cephas before them all, 'If you, though a Jew, live like a gentile and not like a Jew, how can you compel the gentiles to live like Jews?'" This bold confrontation of the reputed spokesman for the Twelve and a major leader of the Jerusalem church contrasts with Paul's reputation elsewhere as someone of meek bodily presence but a strong personality in his letters (2 Cor 10:1). One can only speculate how sharp this confrontation might have been, but the intensity of Paul's feelings indicates that it could have been a tense conversation. It is also clear that Paul thought Peter's actions spoke louder than his words, which is why he is so eager to challenge his duplicitous behavior.

At first glance, Paul's question to Peter seems convoluted, but it becomes clear that "living like a gentile" refers to Peter's having taken table fellowship with gentiles, whereas "to compel the gentiles to live like Jews" is an allusion to observing the Jewish food laws *and* the requirement for circumcision. Paul sees the incongruity of Peter's actions. The verb *anagkazō* ("compel" NABRE, RSV, NRSV; "force" NIV, NET) is the same one used in verse 3 of Titus, who was not forced to be circumcised. So Paul sees some irony in the duplicity as well, in that the rules are not being equally applied.

With his opening defense clearly announced, Paul turns to the main theme of the letter. It may well be a repetition of the kind of explanation Paul gave to Peter for his strong reaction, but here it serves to orient the readers and hearers[9] to the rest of the letter. In this short section, Paul summarizes the essentials of his message for the Galatians. The law has no ability to save people. Rather, salvation only comes from justification by faith in Jesus Christ. It is only through grace that we can be saved.

THE THEME OF THE LETTER: FAITH AND WORKS (2:15–21)

Now Paul comes to the heart of the matter, laying out explicitly for his audience the most important insight that he had gained during his own journey of faith. This is, namely, that doing the regular "works" of the law that was expected of faithful Jews was not required for gentiles. On the contrary, "faith" is what is most important. The language of these two, however, is fraught with a certain amount of ambiguity and ultimately helped to fuel the divisions of Christianity begun in the Protestant Reformation and that persist today. So, we must be careful in our interpretation of Paul's message in order to avoid an exaggerated false dichotomy of works/faith.

¹⁵ We ourselves are Jews by birth and not "gentile sinners"; ¹⁶ yet knowing that a person is justified not by the works of the law but by faith in Jesus Christ. And we have believed in Christ Jesus, so that we may be justified by the faith of Christ, and not by the works of the law, because no human being will be justified by the works of the law. ¹⁷ If, however, in our effort to be justified in Christ, we ourselves also have been found to be sinners, is Christ then a servant of sin? By no means! ¹⁸ For if I build up again the very things that I once tore down, then I show myself to be a transgressor. ¹⁹ For through the law I died to the law, so that I might live to God. I have been crucified with Christ; ²⁰ yet I no longer live, but Christ lives in me. And the life I now live in the flesh I live by faith in the Son of God, who loved me and gave himself for me. ²¹ I do not nullify the grace of God; for if justification comes through the law, then Christ died for nothing.

2:15–16: Ps 143:1–2
2:15–21: Rom 3:21–31; 4:1–5; 8:10–11; 11:6; Eph 2:8–9;
Phil 3:9; Col 3:3–4

The first-person plural, "we," followed by the definition "Jews by nature," shows that this section is almost a continuation of the discussion with Peter. Paul contrasts sharply the traditional Jewish concept of their identity as a chosen, holy people in comparison to the (lit.) "sinners among the gentiles." Those who were born Jews saw themselves as superior to gentiles because of their status as God's chosen people (Deut 7:7–10). They were not like gentiles, the rest of the world! This uncompromising, dualistic attitude was characteristic of the ancient world. The world was divided into Jew or gentile, Greek or barbarian, Roman or pagan (the opposite of Paul's understanding in Gal 3:28). The implication was always that one was better than the other. Paul, however, refers to Jewish Christ believers (like himself) "who know that a person is not justified by works of the law but through faith in Jesus Christ." Peter should thus have known better than to renege on his earlier agreement. Only justification by faith offers salvation, not any fulfillment of the law. Lest there be any doubt, Paul reinforces his point clearly by claiming the reason for his stance: "because no human being will be justified by the works of the law."

Moses Receiving the Tablets of Law by Marc Chagall (ca. 1966 CE)

An open torah scroll

Three expressions in this sentence bear further remark, having occasioned countless pages of discussion over the centuries: What is meant by the verb "justified"; by "works of the law"; and by "faith in Jesus Christ"?

This is the first of eight occurrences of the verb "justify" (*dikaioō*) in Galatians (2:16 [3x], 17; 3:8, 11, 24; 5:4). The same verb occurs fifteen times in Romans, which is thematically close to Galatians, though more extensive and written later. The vocabulary of justification[10] is obviously important to Paul, which he makes clear later in Galatians when he cites the origin of this concept in the figure of Abraham (3:1–6). The verb has a forensic background. It comes from the context of the legal system in which an accused person could be declared righteous or upright, that is, acquitted. Traditionally, Protestants have viewed this as a declaration by God, whereas Catholics have tended to underline the effects of justification, namely, the sinner becomes righteous again. In the past, the danger of the Catholic position had been an overemphasis on the human role in this action, while Protestants have overemphasized the verbal aspect of justification and not the behavioral. Fortunately, ecumenical progress (see sidebar "Justification by Faith in Ecumenical Perspective") has lessened this exaggerated opposition. For Paul, the essential aspect of the concept of being justified is that the source of justification is God. Our human actions are important, but they flow from God's gracious action of justification; they don't earn us this saving action.

This brings us to works of the law. It occurs here for the first time in Galatians but recurs three more times (3:2, 5, 10) and also in Romans (Rom 3:20, 28). The Jewish law (torah) had 613 commandments. That's a lot of regulation. Paul seems to use the phrase "works of the law" as a kind of label, but it is not clear if he is referring to all the regulations of the law or perhaps only to circumcision and the dietary rules, both of which appear in Galatians. Later in the letter, Paul clarifies that the whole law is in view. He asserts that "every man who lets himself be circumcised…is obliged to keep the entire law" (5:3).

Works of the Law

The precise expression "works of the law" is not found in the Hebrew Bible nor in the LXX. It is also absent from the NT except in Paul's letters, where it occurs eight times (Gal 2:16 [3x]; 3:2, 5, 10; Rom 3:20, 28). Paul's use seems to presume a Jewish context in which the expression is well known. There is one occurrence of the Hebrew equivalent in the Dead Sea Scrolls where it refers to "precepts of the law."

There has been a lot of scholarly debate about the precise meaning of "works of the law." Does it mean every commandment and precept of the Jewish law? Does it mean only certain parts of the law? Scholars from the so-called new perspective on Paul propose that the expression really refers to three primary aspects of the law (circumcision, food laws, Sabbath observance) that functioned as "ID badges" for Jews to distinguish them from gentiles. Yet Paul clearly notes that to practice circumcision means obligating oneself to the whole law (Gal 5:3).

A danger in wrongly conceiving of the meaning of "works of the law" is to equate the expression with Jewish legalism as opposed to Christian gospel. This was a standard approach of Protestant Reformers. Modern scholarship has shown that Judaism was not necessarily legalistic, despite its strong emphasis on moral rectitude.

Clearly, Paul juxtaposes works of the law with faith of/in Christ. Paul envisions doing works of the law, understood as all the precepts of the law, as insufficient for Christians because salvation has already, once and for all, been achieved by Christ. "Doing the works of the law" adds nothing to this salvation. Yet living the "law of Christ" under the power of the Holy Spirit results in a righteous and virtuous life (Gal 5:22–23; 6:2).

The problem with the expression "faith in Jesus Christ" (NRSV, NABRE, NIV, NJB) is that the original Greek phrase ("the faith *of* Jesus Christ," NET) is more ambiguous. Once more, the little preposition *of* raises a question. Does it imply that Jesus Christ is the object of our faith, or is it Jesus Christ's own faith, his fidelity, which is meant? Grammatically, both interpretations are possible. This is what scholars call the difference between the objective and subjective genitive. Historically, commentators have understood that Paul conceives of our faith in Christ as the source of justification, but more and more commentators have seen that this puts the emphasis on human action rather than God's action. Thus, gradually, interpreters have moved to an understanding that what Paul has in mind is Christ's fidelity, which is consistent with the rest of Galatians. We should emphasize that these are not totally opposed interpretations. Yet emphasizing Christ's fidelity, especially by his death on a cross, puts the emphasis properly where Paul would have it. Justification is all at the initiative of God's gracious outreach to humanity. Christ's sacrifice on the cross once and for all saved humanity. But that does not absolve us from following up on this gracious act by our own faith *in* the Son of God. That is how Paul's continued explanation fleshes out what he means.

Justification by Faith in Ecumenical Perspective

Since the Protestant Reformation (1517), the topic of justification by faith has been one of the dividing lines between Catholic and non-Catholic teaching on Paul. After the Second Vatican Council (1962–65), however, many dialogues have taken place that have begun to reconsider the division this had caused. Particularly productive has been the series of Lutheran-Catholic dialogues. On the eve of the third Christian millennium, with the approval of Pope John Paul II, the Roman Catholic Church and a large body of Lutherans reached a remarkable accord on the theme of justification. On October 31, 1999 in Augsburg, Germany, a landmark document was signed by official representatives of both denominations. Its key paragraph describes justification by faith in uniform terms:

> In faith we together hold the conviction that justification is the work of the triune God….Together we confess: By grace alone, in faith in Christ's saving work and not because of any merit on our part, we are accepted by God and receive the Holy Spirit, who renews our hearts while equipping and calling us to good works. (*Joint Declaration on the Doctrine of Justification* 15)[11]

An "Annex" issued with the document points out that the agreement does not resolve all the issues of differences of understanding between Lutherans and Catholics on this important Pauline teaching. Yet it does advance and nuance the painstakingly slow process of trying to reunite Christians where divisions have been so strongly wrought. A further encouraging sign occurred in July 2006 in Seoul, South Korea, when the World Methodist Conference voted unanimously to sign the accord as well. The World Communion of Reformed Churches did likewise in Wittenberg, Germany, in July 2017, in part, to mark the five-hundredth anniversary of the Protestant Reformation. So, now four major denominational Christian groups have reached a general accord on the concept of justification by faith. Though much work remains to be done to enhance this ecumenical progress, one can no longer maintain that Protestants and Catholics have a totally different understanding of justification.

Justification in the *Catechism*

Quoting Saint Augustine, the *Catechism* points out why justification is such a great gift from God:

> Justification is the most excellent work of God's love made manifest in Christ Jesus and granted by the Holy Spirit. It is the opinion of St. Augustine that "the justification of the wicked is a greater work than the creation of heaven and earth," because "heaven and earth will pass away but the salvation and justification of the elect…will not pass away." He holds also that the justification of sinners surpasses the creation of the angels in justice, in that it bears witness to a greater mercy. *CCC* §1994. (St. Augustine, *In Jo. ev.* 72, 3: PL 35, 1823)

Paul then asks a rhetorical question that he suspects will be on the Galatians' mind. If we are justified by Christ's fidelity, and if we seek to be justified in Christ by our own faith yet remain sinners, how does justification really work? He asks, "Is Christ then a servant of sin?" To which he adds a resounding denial: "Of course not!" It would be absurd to think that Christ would somehow be a minister of sin just because sinfulness continues in our human existence. But he goes on to say that accepting the law regarding circumcision is not an option once one has accepted the justification that has come in and through Jesus Christ. Switching to the first person "I," through which he means to speak for all Jewish Christians, he says, "For if I build up again those things that I tore down, then I show myself to be a transgressor." He is referring to the dietary laws that he also thinks no longer apply after one is joined to Christ. Reestablishing them once they have been abolished would be another transgression. To which he adds a second reason not to give in to the agitators: "For through the law I died to the law, so that I might live for God." His entrance into Christ, by baptism (see Rom 6:3), which is assumed in the text rather than explicit, enabled Paul to die to the law (see Rom 7:4). Paradoxically, the law is the means for this death ("through the law") because Christ himself died under the law, as Paul notes later (3:13). Indeed, the same verb "die" is used to express Paul's death to the law, that of every Christian, and Christ's death (vv. 19, 21).

Then, almost in the same breath, Paul makes a startling claim: "I have been crucified with Christ." Obviously in this context he uses crucifixion in a metaphorical sense as he does elsewhere (Gal 5:24; 6:14; Rom 6:6), whereas Jesus Christ had literally been crucified (Gal 3:1; see also Mark 15:32; John 19:32; 1 Cor 1:23). The metaphorical sense here, and in 6:14, means that something in him has had to die in order that he could experience the newness of life in Christ. Paul's Christianity is muscular. He recognizes that faith is not easy. One must die to oneself, be crucified with Christ in order to be born into the new creation. By using such strong language, he challenges the Galatians to be ready to do the same thing. They must die to their desire to take refuge or comfort in the law. The law holds no value in terms of salvation; the Galatians should not be seduced into following that path.

Dying to oneself, Paul goes on, leads to life on a whole different level. This new life in Christ is so transforming that it is like living in a different key. One surrenders totally to Christ, with the result that "I no longer live, but Christ lives in me." This is one of the most profound teachings in Galatians because it describes the newness of life that comes about with faith and having been justified. One's very identity is transformed. It is Paul's expression of what the label "Christian" meant when applied to the early followers of Christ (Acts 11:26; contrast 26:28). It basically meant becoming "little Christs." Christ is alive in each and every believer who surrenders to the power of grace. It is living a life that no longer needs the boundaries of law to determine right from wrong, which is why Paul has been insistent that the Galatians not take up that slavery. Once more, though baptism is not named explicitly, this is the essential meaning of this sacrament. Paul is likely reminding the Galatians subtly of their own baptismal transformation they are in danger of abandoning.

The Impact of One Verse

Paul's expression in Galatians 2:20 must be one of the most quoted lines in Christian tradition from the Letter to the Galatians. In the seventeenth century, various spiritual writers from the French school of spirituality quoted it, including Cardinal Pierre de Bérulle, founder of this so-called school of thought. The French school was a seventeenth-century reform movement of holy men and women who desired to improve the sanctity of the church by reforming the clergy. Father Jean-Jacques Olier, another member of the French school and founder of the Society of the Priests of Saint Sulpice, the community of priests to which I belong, was an important figure in the movement. Olier makes it a hallmark of the community he founded for the reform of the clergy:

> The first and last purpose of this Institute [the Sulpicians] will be to live supremely for God in Christ Jesus our Savior, so that the inner life of the Son penetrates the depths of our hearts in a way that permits each one of us to repeat with confidence what St. Paul claimed: "It is no longer I who live, it is Christ who lives in me" (Gal 2:20). (J.-J. Olier, *Pietas Seminarii* §1 [Sulpician Archives, Paris])

The quotation also finds its way into a passage from Vatican II on the priesthood:

> The very holiness of priests is of the greatest benefit for the fruitful fulfillment of their ministry. While it is possible for God's grace to carry out the work of salvation through unworthy ministers, yet God ordinarily prefers to show his wonders through those men who are more submissive to the impulse and guidance of the Holy Spirit and who, because of their intimate union with Christ and their holiness of

life, are able to say with St. Paul: "It is no longer I who live, but Christ who lives in me" (Gal 2:20). (*PO* 12; *PDV* 25)

Paul goes one step further to explain his meaning. Using very personal language, Paul says that "the life I now live in the flesh, I live by faith in the Son of God who has loved me and given himself up for me." In his human existence ("flesh" neutrally understood), he lives "by faith in the Son of God." Here Paul employs exalted language for Christ whom he recognizes as God's Son (Gal 1:16; 4:4; Rom 1:4; 5:10; 1 Cor 1:9). The Greek phrase, however, is again ambiguous and can bear both the emphasis on the Son of God's faithfulness, as well as Paul's personal act of faith, his belief in Jesus Christ as the Son of God. But there is also the unmistakable claim that it was this Son "who has loved me and gave himself up for me." Catholics often shy away from such personal testimony; Evangelical Christians usually find it more familiar. But Paul shows no hesitance here to become very personal. After all, he has based his entire argument thus far on personal authority and experience, especially his call as an apostle. But he is not merely being autobiographical. Essentially, his personal witness speaks for all who have accepted God's outstretched invitation to new life in Christ. Christ died for each one of us personally, but not for us alone as individuals! There is also an essential communal dimension of faith. Paul here uses himself as an example of proper witness, but the goal is to bring his beloved Galatians along the same path.

Finally, Paul rounds out his argument by recalling the contrast between law and justification with which he had introduced his main theme. "I do not nullify the grace of God; for if justification comes through the law, then Christ died for nothing." Using legal language once more, he says he does not nullify God's grace, as one does a will or legal document. Christ's death would be for naught if the law was the proper means of justification. Paul is adamant. Christ's death has been salvific, and its effects continue. Elsewhere he would consider that in the eyes of this world, the cross is folly and absurdity (1 Cor 1:18–25), but for Paul and all who open themselves to this rich gift freely proffered by God, it is not in vain.

PASTORAL AND SPIRITUAL OBSERVATIONS

What is striking about this lengthy passage is Paul's ability to incorporate his own personal history and reflections into his objective teaching. He does not try to hide his checkered past. He knows well that his reputation as a persecutor had preceded him wherever he went on his apostolic mission, especially early on as Barnabas's understudy, and before his own firm reputation as a missionary had been established. But his unwavering confidence in his apostolic call steadied him. He remained confident and set about the task for which he had received his "revelation," namely preaching the good news of Jesus Christ to the gentiles.

We notice, too, that although his call was personal, he acknowledged the role of those whom he knew to be leaders in the nascent community of believers: Cephas, James the brother of the Lord, and John. This is a reminder that ministry is not simply self-indulged. True, one can "feel called" to official ministry, and God can indeed raise up spokespersons for special duties. But, as with Paul, formal ministries within the "church" are usually discerned by proper ecclesial authorities. Some Christian denominations do allow or tolerate auto-proclaimed ministries, but many organized Christian denominations have some form of hierarchical structure that supervises and discerns the authenticity of such "calls." Roman Catholics obviously rely heavily on the structure of the papacy and episcopacy for such discernment. Thus, to be ordained for ministry, one must undergo the numerous steps required that lead to ordination. But such human requirements do not necessarily constrain God's actions.

On this very point, it is startling to see Paul challenge Peter, the spokesman of the Twelve and the acknowledged leader of the Jerusalem community, prior to James the brother of the Lord. The reasons are clear. For Paul, even if recognized authorities try to turn one away from "the truth of the gospel," honest servants of God's word must call them to task. Paul's integrity (with maybe a dose of stubbornness) is what gave him the needed confidence. Note his disdain for hypocrisy here. Paul insists that even the proper authorities should remain honest in their commitment to the gospel message. Wavering or backsliding is not allowed. This had to have made some impression on the Galatians, who were indeed in the same position of backsliding on the gospel that Paul and his colleagues had preached.

A final observation concerns the balance between the personal and theological dimension of Paul's message in this passage. The fact that Galatians 2:19–20 has been cited in spiritual writings repeatedly throughout church history speaks of the importance of this balance. On the one hand, faith is objectively the acknowledgment that in Jesus Christ, salvation was wrought once and for all for the whole world, and we no longer needed to worry about any obligation imposed from the law. On the other hand, recognizing that Christ died for *me*, as well as for all the world, is an extremely flattering and comforting thought. But with it comes Paul's almost mystical insistence of the need to allow Christ to live in us. Once welcomed into the fold of the faith, we no longer live for ourselves (cf. also Rom 14:7). In fact, Paul insists it is Christ who lives in us. He leads us and accompanies us into the new creation.

REFLECTION QUESTIONS

1. Paul brings to bear on his ministry his personal life story. What aspects of your personal life story do you think are pertinent to your faith? Do you feel that God has called you to any specific task? How might your personal gifts and limitations contribute to anything the Lord asks of you?
2. What do you make of Paul's contrast between the human and the divine? How do we discern the two? How do we come to know God's will?

3. What do you make of Paul's expression, "I no longer live but Christ lives in me"? Was this unique to Paul? Do you believe Christ lives in each of us? How can you become "another Christ" in your life?

4. Obviously, the contrast between "works" and "faith" is key to Paul and to this passage. How do you understand both concepts? What is the relationship between the two? Does faith mean never doing "good works"?

5. How do you understand Paul's confrontation with Cephas (Peter)? Was it disrespectful? How, and under what circumstances, should one confront authorities with what one knows to be the truth?

6. Paul affirms the importance of supporting the poor with financial assistance, especially helping the "mother church" of Jerusalem. Do you know of any special obligation among Christians to help one another in this fashion? Is the obligation to help the poor even broader?

7. Paul insists that he does not "nullify the grace of God" (2:21). How could someone nullify God's grace? Is that even possible?

8. What difference does progress in ecumenical discussions, especially between Protestant and Catholics, make today? Are you familiar with such dialogues? What impact have they made in your church? In your life? In the world?

4

FAITH AND FREEDOM
IN CHRIST (3:1–4:31)

In chapter 3, Paul attends to his main concern that the gift of the Holy Spirit brings freedom. At times, his logic can be difficult to follow, but essentially he argues that the Galatians should not abandon this freedom to embrace the law. Paul addresses the arguments of the agitators in Galatia who are trying to seduce them away from the gospel of Jesus Christ. Paul naturally looks to the Scriptures of Israel as a resource, partly, perhaps, because the agitators were doing the same thing. Paul reinforces, however, that his interpretation of the Scriptures, and particularly his focus on the patriarch Abraham, confirms the Galatians' call to freedom.

We can subdivide this lengthy part of the letter's body into six primary sections:

Justification by Faith and the Figure of Abraham (3:1–14)
> Faith and the Spirit (3:1–5)
> Abraham, the Model of Faith (3:6–14)

The Law and the Promise (3:15–22)

What Faith Has Brought (3:23–29)

Freedom in Christ versus Slavery (4:1–11)

Paul's Plea to the Galatians (4:12–20)

An Allegory on Christian Freedom (4:21–31)

The first section (3:1–14) of this part of the body of the letter can be further subdivided into two interrelated sections, verses 1 to 5 and 6 to 14. Both concern faith, but the first treats the issue of the (Holy) Spirit and the second focuses on the figure of Abraham as a model of faith.

JUSTIFICATION BY FAITH AND THE FIGURE OF ABRAHAM (3:1–14)

Faith and the Spirit (3:1–5)

3 [1] O foolish Galatians! Who has bewitched you, before whose eyes Jesus Christ was publicly exhibited as crucified? [2] The only thing I want to learn from you is this: Did you receive the Spirit by doing the works of the law or by believing what you heard? [3] Are you so foolish? Having begun by the Spirit, are you now ending with the flesh? [4] Did you experience so much in vain?—if it really was in vain! [5] Therefore, does the one who gives you the Spirit and works miracles among you do so by the works of the law, or by your believing what you heard?

---

1 Cor 1:23; Rom 4:3; 10:17; Jas 2:23

Paul begins the first subsection (vv. 1–5) with a sharp exclamation: "Foolish Galatians!" The adjective can mean "unthinking" or "lacking perception" or perhaps even "stupid." But it does not refer to a lack of intellectual capacity or moral defect. Rather, it berates the Galatians for squandering their faith. The next sentence indicates that Paul thinks they have allowed themselves to be "bewitched," in the sense of falling under the spell of some curse or devious conversation partners. This must have taken the Galatians by surprise when compared to Paul's earlier familial language ("brothers and sisters" in 1:11). In getting to the heart of the matter, Paul believes there is much at stake, so he must present his argument forcefully to counter the agitators. The force of Paul's statement is, "Are you so foolish?" "Have you lost your minds?"

The reference to the public crucifixion of Jesus is not about the Galatians having physically witnessed it, which of course would have been impossible. Rather, Paul is referring to his preaching of the gospel message (1:6–9), which elsewhere he identifies as essential (see 1 Cor 1:17–18, 23). Paul asks a real question: Who has put you under a spell to lead you away from the gospel of the crucified Christ, the only gospel Paul preached? Paul may not know the precise identity of his opponents, though they are probably identified with similar opponents who favor adhering to the Jewish law as those he mentions who came from James (2:12). Surely, the Galatians themselves know who they are.

Paul then poses a series of rhetorical questions, the first of which concerns his demand to know whether the Galatians' reception of the Spirit was "by doing the works of the law or by believing what you heard." Here, we see Paul's famous contrast between works and faith, which the Reformers made the centerpiece of Paul's teaching on justification. Paul had already tipped his hand about this contrast in the previous section of the letter (2:16) and clearly indicates that the Spirit had been received not through works but through faith.

Crucifixion by Bernardino Luini (ca. 1530 CE)

Here, the expression "believing what you heard" (*ex akoēs pisteōs*) is difficult to translate. The proposed translation follows the NRSV, NIV, REB, and NJB, but NABRE has "faith in what you heard" and the RSV has "hearing with faith." The proposed translation puts the emphasis on the passive reception of the message of the gospel rather than the act of hearing it. Note, however, that Paul acknowledges a role for faith (believing) on the part of Christ followers. Christ's faithfulness saves, but our faith in Christ is an essential response to this grace.

The Holy Spirit in Galatians

Paul does not use the expression "Holy Spirit" in the Letter to the Galatians, though he does elsewhere (see Rom 5:5; 9:1; 1 Cor 6:19; 12:3; 1 Thess 1:5-6; etc.). Rather, he regularly mentions "the Spirit" (Gk. *to pneuma*), which clearly refers to the Holy Spirit except in two instances. One is at the end of the letter, where it refers to the "spirit" of the Galatians in a prayerful wish that Christians still use in worship: "The grace of our Lord Jesus Christ be with your spirit, brothers and sisters" (6:18). In this latter expression, "spirit" refers to the seat of the inner life, or "spiritual" life, of human beings. The other occurrence of "spirit" expresses a human sentiment or attitude of gentleness (6:1).

The study of the role of the Spirit is technically called pneumatology, and it is an important aspect of Paul's overall theological perspective. What do we learn about Paul's pneumatology from Galatians?

The Spirit does not actually make its appearance until chapter 3, where Paul launches into his main topic: faith, freedom, and justification (3:1–6). There he begins with his famous contrast between the Spirit and flesh (*sarx*), contrasting the difference between the life lived according to the values of the Spirit and those lived in accord with the limited and finite perspective of this world (3:3). From there to the end of the letter, Paul invokes the Spirit multiple times to remind the Galatians that the faith they received from God through Paul's preaching is entirely formed by, and maintained by, the Spirit. He wants them to retain this "spiritual" perspective, which can help them understand why following the rule of circumcision would lead them away from Christ, not toward him.

Amid this teaching, Paul affirms the following understanding of the Spirit. God supplies the Spirit (3:5) and sends the Spirit into the heart of each believer so that we can experience true adoption as God's children and be enabled to pray properly, "*Abba*, Father" (4:6). The Spirit is an essential aspect of the Father's promise, who leads us to faith and sustains us in that faith (5:5, 25). This same Spirit is totally opposed to the "flesh" (4:19; 5:16–17) and provides an honest guide for living righteously, not in accordance with the Mosaic law but with the law of Christ, which is rooted in love (5:18). The singular "fruit" of the Spirit is love, which reveals itself in multiple ways through a virtuous life (5:22–23), not through conformity to the law.

In short, in Galatians, Paul affirms the role of the Spirit as a vehicle from God that enables people of faith, by God's own grace, to live in accordance with their baptismal identity. The Spirit is the indispensable companion and guide for life in the new creation.

Paul continues with two more rhetorical questions that he hopes will bring the Galatians to their senses. For a second time he implies their lack of perception. "Are you so foolish?" Do they really want to revert to the flesh once they have received the freedom of the Spirit? This famous Pauline contrast of the flesh and Spirit is reinforced by the natural pairing of the verbs "begun" and "ending" (see also Phil 1:6). The Galatians had begun well in their reception of the Spirit. Paul is concerned that they are ending poorly, by accepting circumcision, which lies behind the image of the flesh here, and which the Galatians wrongly are being led to believe will complete their identity in Christ.

The next rhetorical question is vague. To what does "so much" (*tosauta*, lit. "so many things") refer? To persecutions or suffering? To some, "mighty deeds," as referred to in the next verse? Or perhaps even to the reception of the Spirit? The context favors a reference to the experience of the Spirit, which Paul indicates was not an experience "in vain."

Having begun this section with the contrast between works and the Spirit, Paul concludes it using the same language to contrast "the works of the law" with "believing what you heard." He reinforces the negative consequences for the Galatians if they persist in their folly of following the agitators' advice. In posing the question this way, Paul is attempting to lead the Galatians to the logical answer. It was by the gift of the Holy Spirit that they experienced "miracles" (*dynameis*, lit. "mighty deeds") in their midst, not by works of the law.

Pastoral and Spiritual Observations (3:1–5)

In this section of the letter, Paul is strong in his language concerning the failure of the Galatians by being persuaded to abandon the gospel message. Paul was walking a tightrope. There is risk involved in his argument. Although he had still used familial language earlier in the letter, it must have stung his hearers to be called fools. However, is it not true that we are often seduced by persuasive influences? It is easy to be misled by people who use slick language or attractive images. In fact, one of the sad realities of human existence is how we are persuaded by people who do not tell the truth. We are basically gullible, easily manipulated, willing to believe almost anything packaged in a slick manner and handed on as "the gospel truth." (Remember how important for Paul in Galatians is "the truth of the gospel.") Paul thinks the Galatians have succumbed to this human tendency, which is totally opposed to the truth of his message, which comes from God. So he prepares an all-out offensive to get them back on track.

Reflection Questions

1. What role does the crucifixion of Christ play in Paul's argument? Is it a critical point for him to emphasize? How do you view the crucifixion of Jesus Christ in your faith? How do you make sense of this historical fact?
2. Is it wrong to call someone you perceive to be in danger of abandoning the truth "foolish" or "stupid"? Are there contexts in which such forceful language might be useful and permissible?
3. The contrast between the Spirit and the flesh is foundational for Paul. How would you explain these two concepts to someone interested in the faith today?

Abraham, the Model of Faith (3:6–14)

Having set the stage for his first major argument based on Scripture—especially with the contrast between works and faith—Paul then contrasts the negative consequences with a positive image. He introduces in more detail the patriarch, Abraham, and proposes him as a model of faith—"exhibit A"—of Paul's argumentation, and the heart of Paul's teaching in his Letter to the Galatians. It is likely, however, that the agitators have proposed the same model but not based on faith. Instead, they would have emphasized Abraham's explicit connection to circumcision and thus a mark of the "flesh." For Paul, this is not why

Abraham should be invoked. Abraham is the archetype of faith, and Paul believes followers of Jesus should likewise follow his example. In proposing this model, Paul underlines the contrast between faith and the law. Note, too, that Paul makes extensive use of OT scriptural citations—five in nine verses!—to promote his argument. He shows the importance of familiarity with God's word in laying out the "truth" of his message.

> [6] Just as Abraham "believed God, and it was reckoned to him as righteousness," [7] so, understand, those who have faith are the descendants of Abraham. [8] And the scripture, foreseeing that God would justify the gentiles by faith, proclaimed the gospel beforehand to Abraham, saying, "All the gentiles shall be blessed in you." [9] So then, those who have faith are blessed together with Abraham who believed. [10] For all who rely on the works of the law are under a curse; for it is written, "Cursed is everyone who does not observe and do all the things written in the book of the law." [11] Now it is clear that no one is justified before God by the law; for "the one who is righteous will live by faith." [12] But the law does not come from faith; on the contrary, "Whoever does these things will live by them."
>
> [13] Christ redeemed us from the curse of the law by becoming a curse for us—for it is written, "Cursed is everyone who hangs on a tree"— [14] in order that in Christ Jesus the blessing of Abraham might come to the gentiles, so that we might receive the promise of the Spirit through faith.

**Gen 12:3; 15:6; 18:17–19; 22:17–18; 26:3–4; 28:13–14;
Lev 18:5; Deut 21:23; 27:26
Rom 1:17; 10:5; Jas 2:10**

*The Three Angels Visiting Abraham,
from the Story of Abraham*
by Georg Pencz (ca. 1500–1550 CE)

In the next subsection (3:6–14), some interpreters regard verse 6 as the conclusion of the previous section (NEB, NABRE). This is feasible, but it seems best to consider it the opening of the extended scriptural image of Abraham and his significance. The first words, "just as" (*kathōs*), can mean "likewise" or "in the same way," and here they begin a comparison. It introduces a direct quote from the LXX (Gen 15:7) that is a crucial verse for Paul. Abraham is the model of faith because he "believed God, and it was reckoned to him as righteousness." The line comes from the passage in Genesis (15:1–7) where God invites Abraham into a covenantal relationship. Importantly, this is not the OT passage of the covenant of circumcision (Gen 17:1–14) but rather the promise of innumerable descendants, despite Abraham and Sarah's old age. For Paul, Abraham's simple yet profound act of faith is what is striking, not his later association with the covenant of circumcision. He accepts the Lord's promise without question or debate, despite appearances that could call into question the validity or credibility of God's word. Consequently, God reckons or "credits" (NABRE, NET) it to him as "righteousness."

Abraham

Abraham is one of the most important figures from the OT. Considered today the father of three monotheistic faiths (Judaism, Christianity, Islam), Abraham was already a model of upright religious belief in OT times. The Book of Sirach, for instance, describes him as a model for observance of the law, although he existed before the law of Moses came into being:

> Abraham was the great father of a multitude of nations,
> and no one has been found like him in glory.
> He kept the law of the Most High,
> and entered into a covenant with him;
> he certified the covenant in his flesh,
> and when he was tested he proved faithful.
> Therefore the Lord assured him with an oath
> that the nations would be blessed through his offspring;
> that he would make him as numerous as the dust of the earth,
> and exalt his offspring like the stars. (Sir 44:19-21 NRSV)

For Paul, however, Abraham's significance is not rooted in his obedience to the law but in his initial faith when God instructed him to move himself and his family to the area now referred to as the Holy Land. Paul uses many aspects of the Abraham story in the explanation of his gospel message. Despite the covenant of circumcision with Abraham (Gen 17:1-7), Paul calls Abraham "the ancestor of all who believe without being circumcised and who thus have righteousness reckoned to them" (Rom 4:11 NRSV).

Paul's use of the image of Abraham in Galatians is crucial to his argument, since the Galatians were receiving a message from Paul's opponents about being a model of law observance—and circumcision—rather than faith. For Paul, Abraham the man of faith, not the law observer, is what is essential.

Since Abraham is the ideal model of faith for Paul, he proceeds to speak of "those who have faith" ("those who believe," NRSV) as "descendants" of Abraham (lit. "sons of Abraham"). Although the masculine image of sonship is prominent in this section of the letter, Paul clearly understands the inheritance from Abraham as intended for all believers, women and men alike (see 3:26–29). Thus "descendants" is a valid translation for the sake of inclusivity.

Paul uses the generic expression "scripture" to represent the whole of the OT, but he virtually personifies Scripture (also 3:22) with the expression "foreseeing," envisioning Scripture as a living tradition that affects contemporary life. Paul cites a passage from Gen 12:3 of the Abraham story to show that the justification of the gentiles was already foreseen in the promise to Abraham that "all the gentiles shall be blessed in you." The expression "gentiles" (*ethnē*) can also be translated "nations" (NABRE, NJB, NIV), which is the emphasis in the Abraham story (see Gen 18:18), but here the context concerns Paul's overarching argument about the gentiles not needing to become Jews to have faith in Jesus. Paul's vivid understanding of the power of Scripture is reinforced by his assertion that Scripture had "proclaimed the gospel beforehand" ("in advance," NIV) "to Abraham." Although, by his analogy, Paul is not making Abraham a follower of Christ, a "Christian" in our language, he envisions strong continuity between the Scriptures of old and the gospel or good news of Jesus Christ.[1] In fact, here Paul envisions a "salvation history" in which God's gracious action, begun in Abraham, finds its supreme fulfillment in Jesus Christ who, as the new or "last Adam" (1 Cor 15:45), brings a new creation into being.

Paul's simple conclusion ("so then," or "consequently," NABRE) is then stated. Those who have faith (in Jesus Christ) are equally blessed as faithful Abraham, using the adjective "faithful" (*pistos*), which Paul uses less frequently than forms of the verb "believe" (*pisteuō*).

Carrying his argument further, Paul connects "works of the law" with being "under a curse," because it will serve his contrast between Abraham, the model believer, and those who are under the law. He uses another quotation[2] from the LXX (Deut 27:26), with modest changes, that demonstrates that not performing every detail of the law makes one cursed. Why? Because accepting the law, with all its 613 prescriptions, obliges one to fulfill every aspect of it, and not accomplishing it makes one cursed rather than blessed.

Then Paul states that "no one is justified before God by the law," using a citation from Habakkuk he also employs in Romans (1:17): "The one who is righteous will live by faith" (Hab 2:4, though not with exact wording from either the LXX or the Hebrew Bible). It furthers the contrast between the law and faith.

Again, quoting from Scripture—this time from Leviticus, and not with precise wording from the LXX or Hebrew Bible—Paul asserts that "the law does not come from faith," in the sense of its origin. Rather, the law demands the observance of all its precepts. The ambiguous phrase "these things" likely refers to the works of the law. Faith thus lies in a different category altogether.

Paul's Use of Scripture

One cannot read Paul's letters without noticing the frequent use of Scripture, either in quotation or allusion, though the latter is much harder to identify. Paul cites Scripture a little over one hundred times (not counting bona fide allusions), almost always using the Septuagint rather than the Masoretic text of the Hebrew Bible. As a diaspora Jew, in fact, Paul would have been very familiar with the Greek version of the OT. Most of the citations are found in his letters to the Romans (60x), 1 Corinthians (17x), 2 Corinthians (10x), and Galatians (10x), where we find many crucial aspects of Paul's theological perspective. Paul's source books from the OT are also restricted. The four most frequently cited books are Isaiah (25x), Psalms (19x), Genesis (15x), and Deuteronomy (15x).

Why does he cite Scripture? As with all Jews, Paul believed the Sacred Scriptures of Israel were God's living word (see Rom 1:2; 15:4). The OT thus had perennial value. He cites it liberally as part of his argumentation, especially when he believes it bolsters his point of view. Paul thus tends to use Scripture for "proof texting"—proving his point by quoting an authoritative, inspired text. The agitators in Galatians, however, were engaged in the same enterprise, so Paul was, in a sense, forced to play the same game. As we will note, Paul at times takes liberties with his interpretation of OT texts in ways that we would consider bending the Scriptures in an extremely creative way. But this was not an unusual practice among rabbis of the day. (See the sidebar "Paul and Rabbinic Method.")

The study of biblical citations in the Bible (formally called "intertextuality") has produced a flood of recent publications. For an introduction, see Moyise.

Verses 13–14 are one long sentence in Greek through which Paul weaves together several ideas he has been exploring in this section. He plays off the vocabulary of "curse" to assert a paradox, namely, that "Christ redeemed us from the curse of the law by becoming a curse for us." The verb "redeemed" (*exagorazō*) means to pay a price to buy someone back from slavery (see also 4:5). It comes out of a context whereby captives from warfare were regularly sold into slavery. To be freed, they had to be bought back. Thus Paul is affirming that Christ paid a price to buy us from the obligation of adhering to the law in all its precepts. He did this paradoxically by himself becoming a curse. The OT quotation from Deuteronomy explains why: "Cursed is everyone who hangs on a tree" (21:23). Originally, the saying referred to the hanging of corpses of deceased criminals on trees as a deterrent to crime. Over time the expression became a reference to the ignominious death by crucifixion, a type of "hanging" (being impaled) on wood.

The Significance of the Crucifixion

Saint Jerome (ca. 340-420), the famous biblical exegete and translator who also wrote commentaries, explains the significance of Jesus's death on a cross:

> He died so that we might live. He descended into Hades so that we might rise to heaven. He became foolish so that we might become wise. He emptied himself of the fullness and forms of God and assumed the form of a servant so that the fullness of divinity might dwell in us and so that we might go from being servants to masters. He hung on a tree so that by means of a tree he might erase the sin we had committed through the tree of knowledge of good and evil. (Jerome, *Commentary on Galatians*, 144.)

In this humble action, the redemptive act of Christ is explained by two purpose clauses (introduced by the same Greek word). The first purpose is so that "in Christ Jesus the blessing of Abraham might come to the gentiles." Christ is thus the means through which the blessing of Abraham can be extended even to the gentiles. But the second purpose is even more inclusive: "so that we might receive the promise of the Spirit through faith." The "we" refers both to Jews and gentiles, for both are the recipients of "the promise of the Spirit" that comes with faith. The word "promise" (*epangelian*) hints at a major theme for the rest of the chapter and into chapter 4 of the letter. Paul will emphasize that God is faithful to God's promise, of which the Galatians themselves are recipients, if they don't allow it to slip away from them by their own foolishness.

Thus far, Paul has been stern in his tone toward the Galatians, but by continuing to address them in this section as "brothers and sisters," he tries to moderate his voice to gain a more favorable hearing. Since he has been working with the image of Abraham, and has also employed the notion of "promise," Paul now explains how this works in practical terms. The contrast continues through the concepts of law and promise.

THE LAW AND THE PROMISE (3:15–18)

[15] Brothers and sisters, let me speak from a human perspective: once a person's will has been ratified, no one adds to it or annuls it. [16] Now the promises were

made to Abraham and to his descendant; it does not say, "and to descendants," as concerning many; but it says, "and to your offspring," that is, to one person, who is Christ. [17] My point is this: the law, which came 430 years later, does not revoke a covenant previously ratified by God, so as to nullify the promise. [18] For if the inheritance comes from the law, it no longer comes from the promise; but God graciously gave it to Abraham through the promise.

[19] Why then the law? It was added because of transgressions, until the descendant would come to whom the promise had been made; and it was ordained through angels by the hand of a mediator. [20] Now a mediator involves more than one party; but God is one. [21] Therefore is the law opposed to the promises of God? By no means! For if a law had been given that was able to give life, then righteousness would indeed come through the law. [22] But the scripture imprisoned all under the power of sin, so that what was promised by faith in Jesus Christ might be given to those who believe.

Gen 12:1–4, 7; 13:15; 15:1–6; 17:8; 22:17; 24:7; Exod 12:40
Matt 1:1; Rom 3:9–20, 23; 4:13–16; 7:7–10; 11:6;
    Heb 9:16–17
Deut 6:4
Acts 7:38–53; Rom 3:9–20, 23; 4:13–16; 8:2–4

In this section (3:15–18), Paul tries to convince the Galatians about his perspective by taking an example from everyday life (lit. "from a human perspective").[3] He offers the notion of a person's "will," their testament (*diathēkē*). He knows well how controversial last testaments can sometimes be. How many times have wills divided families? Disputes can quickly arise, especially if there has been any suspected tampering with the will. Once it has been "ratified, no one adds to it or annuls it." To do so would jeopardize its validity. We should be careful not to read this line too literally since wills can be modified or even abrogated under certain circumstances. Under normal circumstances, however, a will stands as one's last testament.

Likewise, Abraham's inheritance, here expressed by the plural "promises" (Gen 17:1–9), refers to God's promises "to Abraham and to his descendant" (lit. "to his seed"). Paul, in a very nuanced interpretation of the Genesis passage, pointedly notes the singular form "seed," rather than the plural. The word in Genesis (LXX) is a *collective* noun (*spermati*), which can be understood as singular or plural. Paul, however, applies it directly to Christ, the sole inheritor, an innovative application of the Genesis reading.

Paul appreciates that what he has thus far asserted about the law must raise questions in the minds of the Galatians. If the law is so limited and indeed so bad that it can even be called a curse, then why did it exist in the first place? He thus explains both the limitations of the law and the purpose it served.

Paul and Rabbinic Method

Modern readers often struggle with Paul's use of Scripture. It is helpful to keep in mind that his approach was largely consistent with the typical way the rabbis of his day approached the Scriptures, which is different from our own methods. In Galatians, for instance, several passages show that Paul's approach is not our own.

In verses 10–14, Paul's argumentation about the law not depending on faith can be hard to follow, especially when he toys with the word "curse" and then shows it in contrast to the "promise." Another case is his complicated use of the word "will" (which also means "testament") in verses 15–18 and applying it to God's promise to Abraham, fulfilled through his "descendant," once more using a loose interpretation of the word in the original text. Or yet again, his extended allegory of the two women and the two Jerusalems (see 4:21–31).

In such instances, the rabbis often interpreted the Scriptures in a much broader fashion. They used ideas like "typology," in which some OT passages provided a "type" or "model" of later passages (e.g., Rom 5:14); "fulfillment," where prophetic passages were fulfilled in specific instances; or "catchwords," which connected otherwise unrelated passages by words that appeared in a new context, or even using figures like Abraham, Adam, or Moses in creative ways, as Paul does in Galatians. Such applications were typical of Jewish interpretation of his day, and Paul was certainly trained in such methods. While his manipulation of some passages may strike us as too freewheeling, it would have probably struck his readers in Galatia as typical; the agitators probably used similar methods as well.

In fact, Paul would probably have expected the gentiles to know his allusions to Scripture. While they may not have had as much background as Paul, and perhaps could not follow all the nuances of the argumentation, the Scriptures featured prominently in the preaching of all the apostles, and even gentile converts would be expected to know a fair amount (e.g., the expression, "do you not know" in Rom 6:16; 7:1).

His first explanation, although contorted from a modern reader's perspective, is that the law came 430 years after the promises (the time of Moses by ancient reckoning, Exod 12:40), not to revoke the covenant nor to nullify the promise, but "because of transgressions" (v. 19). While the phrase "because of transgressions" is ambiguous, the context indicates that the purpose of the law was to help people identify transgressions. It was a measuring stick, a way to know right from wrong, and Paul states that it served this purpose properly for a time, not to promote sin but to help in identifying it "until the descendant [Christ] would come to whom the promise [singular] had been made" (v. 19). He further explains that the law came through a mediator (Moses),[4] also making an obscure reference to "angels" (perhaps alluding to Moses's time with God on Mount Sinai, where he received the law). But these figures do not take the place of "God" who is "one." God alone was the source of the law, but the law did not and could not bring "righteousness" (v. 21). Rather, "scripture," here representing God's will, "imprisoned all under the power of sin" (see also Rom 11:32), so that the promise that comes from "the faith of Jesus Christ" (here understood as Christ's own faithfulness) could be given to believers.

Certainly, a complex argument, but Paul is essentially reminding the Galatians that Christ is the true heir, the one who receives the promise that began with Abraham. The law was only temporary and thus has no permanent value for the Galatians who are called to faith, not law observance. He goes on to expand this very point, concluding again with the image of Abraham.

WHAT FAITH HAS BROUGHT US (3:23-29)

[23] Now before faith came, we were detained under the law, and imprisoned until the coming faith would be revealed. [24] Therefore the law was our disciplinarian until Christ came, so that we might be justified by faith. [25] But now that faith has come, we are no longer under a disciplinarian, [26] for you are all children of God through faith in Christ Jesus. [27] As many of you as were baptized into Christ have clothed yourselves with Christ. [28] There is no longer Jew or Greek, there is no longer slave or free, there is no longer male and female; for all of you are one in Christ Jesus. [29] And if you are Christ's, then you are Abraham's descendants, heirs according to a promise.

> Rom 4:16–17; 6:3–4; 8:14–17; 10:4, 12; 13:14; 1 Cor 12:13;
> Eph 4:24; Col 3:11; John 1:12

In this next brief section (3:23–29), Paul adds another image to his explanation of the law so that he can contrast it with faith. The law temporarily "imprisoned and guarded" us until faith would arrive. It functioned as a "disciplinarian" (*paidagōgos*, lit. "pedagogue"; "custodian," RSV; "a slave to look after us," NJB), a familiar image in Paul's day. The term refers to a trusted slave who would watch over children until they were of age, often accompanying them to school or the gymnasium, both protecting them, ensuring they got there, and instructing them in certain skills. Therefore, the law was like a disciplinarian/guardian for a time. But now, says Paul to the Galatians, "you are all children [lit. 'sons'] of God through faith." There is no longer need for a disciplinarian. He recalls the strong image of baptism and the profound change in status that it brings. We are "clothed" with Christ (see also Eph 4:24; Col 3:10), and all become one. Baptism into Christ is like putting on a new set of clothes; it changes us completely, so much so that our usual means of self-identity (Jew/Greek, slave/free, male/female) no longer hold. (The metaphorical use of "clothing" oneself is also an OT image; see Pss 35:26; 132[131]:18; Job 8:22).

These striking contrasts in identity (v. 28) deserve some comment: "There is no longer Jew or Greek, there is no longer slave or free, there is no longer male and female; for all of you are one [person] in Christ Jesus." A more universal view of humankind can scarcely be imagined. Yet, at what level does Paul intend this sentence? Surely, Paul's churches were not totally egalitarian. Some hierarchy seems to have existed, or at the very least, division of labor in ministry (see 1 Cor 12:27–30). Note, also, that the conjunction in the expression "male and female" is *and*, not *or*. Paul here evokes the Creation story where God created the human person "male *and* female" (Gen 1:28). Paul sees in baptism, and in the birth of a new family of faith, a totally new creation (Gal 6:15) in which humanity will once again have the chance to be unified (and not divided) as God intended. Sociologically, Paul's churches surely still had divisions (such as at Corinth, 1 Cor 1:10–17), some of which may have been the result of ethnic identity, socioeconomic differences, gender, and stereotypical roles in society. Yet ideally, Paul thinks that all believers are equally heirs of the promise: "for all of you are one [person] in Christ Jesus" (v. 28). In a world that tended to divide people into two categories (Jew/gentile; circumcised/uncircumcised; slave/free; Roman/barbarian; man/woman), Paul's message would have been startling.[5] (Are we that far removed in our day from a similarly dualistic, divisive worldview?) He then clinches his argument by connecting Christ with Abraham. If you belong to Christ (lit. "are of Christ"), then you are Abraham's "offspring [*sperma*], heirs according to the promise."

What Paul accomplishes in this meaty section of his letter is remarkable. With the backdrop of baptism and the new identity in Christ that comes to believers, he reminds the Galatians of all they are in danger of losing if they listen to, and follow up on, the urgings of the agitators. He uses the latter's own model, Abraham, to counter, step-by-step, their seduction of the Galatians. Abraham's value is that he was a man of faith, a believer. He trusted God without question. He accepted God's promise. As Paul continues his argument in the next section, he will again appeal to certain scriptural texts concerning Abraham, reading them through his own lens to reinforce his point by focusing on the "inheritance" due to people of faith.

PASTORAL AND SPIRITUAL OBSERVATIONS (3:1–29)

In this section of the letter, Paul begins to marshal his arguments to convince the Galatians not to succumb to the agitators' attempts to sway them from the truth of the gospel. He immediately invokes the Spirit, because all who have been reborn in Christ have received the Spirit. The Holy Spirit is the one who sustains our Christian identity. In the Spirit, we can accomplish all good deeds, not in fulfillment of the law, but because they show that we have accepted the new life Christ has offered by his death and resurrection. But Paul knows he needs some persuasive evidence beyond his own ingenuity. He turns to the Scriptures, where he finds the obvious model: Abraham.

Likely, as noted above, the agitators were also using Abraham, but for the opposite argument. Because he is the origin of the covenant of circumcision—the action through which Israel was granted its unique identity as God's chosen people—they were promoting this same practice. But Paul sees a deeper message in the Abraham story. He quotes the key line that emphasizes Abraham's pure faith, the obedient following of God's will: "Abraham 'believed God, and it was reckoned to him as righteousness'" (3:6). Faith is key, not adherence to the law. Moreover, Paul brings the cross into focus, for by it, salvation has been wrought. It is the seal of Christ's faithfulness. We have been "redeemed from the curse of the law" (3:13). Since God's promise to Abraham was to be the father of a multitude, Paul sees this promise fulfilled in the gentiles (which can also be translated as the "nations"). The promise comes through Abraham but continues to our own day. All who are baptized share in this inheritance through Christ, the primary "descendant" of Abraham, the one in whom true fidelity has been seen.

We might well ask why Paul takes such a strong view against the law. He recognizes its value. He admits that it accomplished a good goal for a time, just as a good tutor does for a beginning student. Law helps us know right from wrong, and it helps people set limits and establish expectations. But law can also lead in various directions that are dead ends. Think, for instance, of those who succumb to scrupulosity or legalism, or who become fearful of ever making a false move. There are those, too, who are overwhelmed by the thought of observing so many regulations. They cannot keep sight of the bigger picture. Law can stifle one's spirit.

So Paul offers a different vision, one based upon the transformation by God's grace that happens in baptism. We are clothed anew in Christ. We become new beings. We do not need to ask where the boundaries of proper behavior are because we enter a new family of relationships in which old distinctions—such as, slave/free, gentile/Jew, woman/man—no longer apply. All are "one" in Christ. All support the new life because all have received the same Spirit as a trustworthy guide.

Paul's vision sounds all too neat. Did he really believe that such human divisions simply fell away once one entered the family of faith? Did slavery, gender bias, or fear of outsiders simply disappear? Unlikely, at least from a sociological viewpoint. Paul's communities, like our own today, still evidenced divisions and cliques (e.g., the Corinthians). Consider the divisions in the world today: ethnic, political, sexual orientation, economic, and so on. Christ's death on the cross, and his vindication in the resurrection, have not literally changed daily life in the world. Yet, in the new creation, a new world order is supposed to take hold. For Paul and for all believers, it is the definitive turning point in which the world's only hope exists. If nothing else, Paul gives us a marvelous vision of what life in the new creation should and must be, and he called upon the Galatians to embrace it and put it into action. The task remains the same today.

REFLECTION QUESTIONS

1. In your own words, explain the contrast between works of the law and faith. Are they absolute opposites? If not, what is their relationship?
2. Why did Paul use the Abraham story from Genesis? What aspects of Abraham do you personally find attractive as a model of faith? Do you see any downside to the image of Abraham?
3. According to Paul, what was the original purpose of God's law (torah)? Why does he now hold that it no longer applies in the same way for his gentile converts as it did for Jews? Does this mean there is no value to the law? Why do we still quote the Ten Commandments (Exod 20:1–17) today if there is no value to the law?
4. What role does baptism play in this section of Paul's letter? How important is the sacrament of baptism to Christian identity? Has your baptism made a difference in your life? Do you recall the significance of your baptism from time to time, or was it simply a one-time event that no longer affects your life?
5. Galatians 3:28 is a dramatic statement that human divisions have ceased for those who are "in Christ." Does this now mean that everyone is equal? If so, how, and if not, why not?

FREEDOM IN CHRIST VERSUS SLAVERY (4:1–11)

4 ¹ So this is my point: as long as the heir is a child, he is no better than a slave, even though he is the master of everything; ² rather, he remains under guardians and managers until the date set by the father. ³ So it is with us; when we were children, we were enslaved by the elemental spirits of the world. ⁴ But when the fullness of time had come, God sent his Son, born of a woman, born under the law, ⁵ in order that he might redeem those under the law, so that we might receive adoption. ⁶ And because you are children, God has sent the Spirit of his Son into our hearts, crying, "*Abba*! Father!" ⁷ So you are no longer a slave but a child, and if a child then also an heir, through God.

⁸ But formerly, when you did not know God, you were enslaved to beings that by nature are not gods. ⁹ However, now that you have come to know God—or rather to be known by God—how can you turn back again to the weak and impotent elemental spirits? Do you want to be enslaved to them all over again? ¹⁰ You

observe special days, and months, and seasons, and years. [11] I am afraid that I may have labored for you in vain!

Continuing his discussion of faith and freedom, Paul turns again in this chapter to a legal image, the "heir." Using the image of a child, he develops his argument, over three subsections, to show that the Galatians are not slaves but rightful heirs. The first (vv. 1–11) uses the analogy of slaves/heirs in the cultural context of the Jewish and Greco-Roman worlds of Paul's day. The second (vv. 12–20) presents a personal appeal to the Galatians to come to their senses. The final section (vv. 21–31) offers another detailed scriptural allegory on Christian freedom, using Paul's favorite model of righteousness, the patriarch Abraham.

Heirs, not Slaves

Paul first expands his argument from the previous chapter. He develops the analogy of the child who is the rightful heir of his father, not a slave. The NRSV's use of the plural here, as opposed to the singular in Greek (*klēromonos*, "heir"; see v. 7; also NAB), somewhat obscures Paul's rhetoric because behind the argument lies the figure of Christ, a model Son and heir (see 3:16).

Slavery in Paul's World

Slavery in the NT is a complex topic. At times, the language of slavery is used in a literal sense, referring to those who are owned by masters and thus are not free men and women (1 Cor 7:21-22; Eph 6:5; Col 3:22; Titus 2:9). Even though Paul does not attack the institution of human slavery, which the Christian churches would only confront in the nineteenth century, he nonetheless held that slaves had the same human dignity as those who are free (Gal 3:28; Eph 6:8; Col 3:25). Moreover, when it came to slaves becoming Christians, Paul urged their acceptance as "brothers and sisters" and no longer as slaves (Phlm 16-17), something that would likely have been perceived as seditious in a society built upon a structure of slaves and masters.

In relationship to Christ, however, Paul turns the concept on its head and makes of it an honorific title used of himself (Rom 1:1), his fellow workers (Phil 1:1; Col 1:7; 4:7), and all who would follow Jesus Christ (1 Cor 7:22).[6] Ironically, slavery to Christ is ultimately freeing. Servitude in this manner is to humble oneself as Christ did and to serve others (Phil 2:7; see also John 13:14-15; Rom 6:22; 7:25; Mark 10:43-44).

In Galatians, as in Romans, Paul's concept of being a slave of Christ supports his insistence that once freed from the slavery of sin and the law, followers of Jesus Christ should never submit again. Rather, they become free "children" of God who are no longer slaves but heirs, yet who paradoxically surrender themselves as servants of God and his Messiah (Gal 4:7-11; Rom 6:22; 7:25; cf. John 15:15).

Roman collared slaves

All children need supervision, and Paul recalls a common practice of his day wherein the obedient heir remained "under guardians and managers until the date set by the father." Paul alludes to the disciplinarian or pedagogue he had mentioned earlier (3:25). He presses his image, applying it to the Galatians, and to himself (v. 3 "we," emphatic in Greek). Everyone recognizes instances when, as immature children or adolescents, we were under the influence of external powers—for example, from peer pressure or perhaps desire for worldly things such as money, goods, influence, power, and the like—and needed guidance. Thus, children are "managed" for a time until they come of age, then a parent hopes their upbringing will allow them to make their way in the world without too many pitfalls.

In this context, Paul's mention of enslavement to "the elemental spirits of the world" has long puzzled commentators (see Gal 4:3, 9; Col 2:8, 20). What precisely are they? Since antiquity, various proposals have been made. Two factors indicate that these images likely refer to the elements of the world, which some ancients thought controlled nature.

First, the OT Wisdom literature itself refers to the attraction of astrological signs and the basic elements of the world (earth, air, water, fire; see Wis 7:17–19; 13:1–3; de Boer, 252–56). Second, in the context of Galatians, Paul distinguishes between "the present evil age," under the influence of evil forces, and the age to come (1:4). Until that new age arrives, with its "Jerusalem above" (4:26), there is a danger of succumbing to the powers of this world. Paul warns the Galatians that they risk reverting to these pagan practices, which were not unknown even in the Jewish world.[7]

Paul then interjects a subtle reference to what we call the doctrine of the incarnation[8] to support his paternal imagery. At just the right time (see also Mark 1:15; Eph 1:10),[9] God, acting like a gracious Father, "sent his Son, born of a woman." If Paul's teaching on the incarnation does not have the poetic breadth of the Fourth Gospel's Word-made-flesh (see John 1:1–18), it is no less profound, emphasizing Jesus's full humanity. Like all human beings, Jesus had a mother!

Mary's Role in Salvation History

Some may find it curious that Paul never mentions Mary, the mother of Jesus, who is subtly referred to in Galatians 4:4. This is not surprising, however, since Paul also has little information about Jesus of Nazareth as recorded in the canonical Gospels. Paul's interest is in Christ Jesus, the risen Lord. This little reference in Galatians, however, can be considered Paul's input on the doctrine of the incarnation. He acknowledges Jesus as "born of a woman" and "born under the law." This happened "in the fullness of time," an expression that indicates the history of salvation, in which things happen in accord with God's holy timeframe.

As Christian history developed and reflection upon Mary's role deepened, the Church expanded its understanding of Mary's role in this divine history. Two citations from the *Catechism of the Catholic Church*, both of which refer to Galatians 4:4, illustrate this development:

> The Annunciation to Mary inaugurates "the fullness of time,"[10] the time of the fulfillment of God's promises and preparations. Mary was invited to conceive him in whom the "whole fullness of deity" would dwell "bodily."[11] (*CCC* §484)
>
> "God sent forth his Son," but to prepare a body for him,[12] he wanted the free cooperation of a creature. For this, from all eternity God chose for the mother of his Son a daughter of Israel, a young Jewish woman of Nazareth in Galilee, "a virgin betrothed to a man whose name was Joseph, of the house of David; and the virgin's name was Mary."[13]
>
> The Father of mercies willed that the Incarnation should be preceded by assent on the part of the predestined mother, so that just as a woman had a share in the coming of death, so also should a woman contribute to the coming of life.[14] (*CCC* §488)

Paul, however, sees a paradox in this divine scenario. God's Son, Jesus Christ, is "born under the law." In other words, he was subjected to the same law as all Jews. But his coming was not to promote enslavement to the law. Rather, the Son came for redemption (the verb *exagorazō*, lit. "buy back") from the law and to bestow the dignity of adoption as an heir. Christ's coming into the world as a human being (see Phil 2:7) was to redeem all those under the power of the law, including Paul and the Galatians ("we" in v. 5).

It is worth noting here the biblical and Greco-Roman notions of adoption (*hyiothesia*, a legal term used in the NT only in the Pauline letters; see Rom 8:14, 23; 9:4; Eph 1:5). The Hebrew Bible rarely speaks of adoption in the sense of the later Greco-Roman practice. The law does not mention it. (Being childless, in the OT, normally prepares for miraculous conceptions rather than adoptions, e.g., Sarai [Gen 16:1–4] or Rachel [Gen 29:31–35].) Rather, the OT employs the terminology metaphorically, for example, in God's adoption of the king as a son (see Ps 2:7; 2 Sam 7:14; Jer 3:19). Nevertheless, the desire to have progeny— especially a son to carry on the family identity—was every father's heartfelt hope (e.g., Pss 45:16; 127:3–4). Yet not all parents had children. By Paul's day, a "father's" adoption of a "son" had become a common practice in the Greco-Roman world. One sometimes adopted a nephew or other relative, or even a beloved freed slave, to ensure an heir (e.g., Pliny the Elder adopting his nephew Pliny the Younger). The practice of making a will usually accompanied this process. Adopted sons could neither be repudiated nor enslaved, nor could they be reclaimed by natural parents. They became authentic heirs. Paul, of course, uses the expression here as a metaphor, and it need not be restricted by gender, but refers to all who are "adopted" by God through baptism. Yet it shows the seriousness of the matter. God, like a father adopting a son, makes us genuine children, and thus true heirs, not subject to the law, not enslaved, but freely given our identity by a Father whose love transcends the physical and blood boundaries of family.

As his thought progresses, Paul's nascent trinitarian perspective emerges subtly. Only by (God's) Spirit can we cry out as children, "*Abba*! Father!" Quoting the Aramaic word *Abba* (an intimate expression akin to "Dad," translating it with its Greek equivalent, "Father" [*ho patēr*]; see Mark 14:36; Rom 8:15), Paul recalls Jesus's own intimate style of prayer to his Father (see Matt 6:9; 26:39, though lacking the Aramaic word). Jesus shared this practice with his disciples, now preserved in the Lord's Prayer (see also Luke 11:2). Recall also the relationship of a loving father to his beloved son.

Paul draws this part of his analysis to a clear conclusion: "So you are no longer a slave but a child, and if a child then also an heir through God." The final verses (8–11) reinforce his argument. He harks back to the Galatians' prebaptism days, "when you did not know God." They acted typically as pagans, those who do not know the one true God (see Jer 10:25; Ps 79:6; 1 Thess 4:5). Paul reiterates what he knows is both a basic human temptation and Israel's own habitual flaw—idolatry, the primal sin of all human beings since Adam (see Gen 3:22–24; Exod 32:1–35). We, the creatures, make ourselves gods! Being a true child and heir of God's promise means leaving all such behavior behind. The Galatians' baptismal identity has bestowed upon them sonship (i.e., being sons and daughters of God the Father). Paul is not so subtly indicating that they should "grow up" and act in accordance with their new baptismal identity.

Paul also briefly affirms the Galatians' faith, but quickly corrects himself, wanting to keep the emphasis on the divine initiative. He asks them sincere questions about why they would want to turn to antiquated behavior as slaves, given the dignified identity as divine heirs they have received by faith. He even expands his understanding of the idolatry the Galatians are practicing. He accuses them of *presently* "observing special days, and months, and seasons, and years" (present tense), something also practiced among the Jews of his day (see Col 2:16; and also Num 10:10; 28:14; Amos 8:5; 1 Macc 10:34). Likely the agitators from Jerusalem had brought along some of these practices with their message of circumcision and law-observant behavior, trying to entice the Galatians to their version of the Christian faith. Paul regards it all as idolatry, to be forcefully rejected.

At the end of this part of his argument, with almost an air of defeat and disappointment, Paul admits, "I am afraid that I may have labored for you in vain." He is like a parent watching a child dissipate his or her future by succumbing to childish behavior! He is on the verge of thinking that all his efforts as founder and evangelizer have gone down the drain. But he does not give up. Rather, he launches a more personal emotional appeal.

PAUL'S PLEA TO THE GALATIANS (4:12–20)

[12] Brothers and sisters, I beg you, become as I am, for I also have become as you are. You have done me no wrong. [13] Now you know that it was due to an illness of mine that I first preached the gospel to you; [14] though my condition was a trial for you, you did not scorn or despise me, but welcomed me as an angel of God, like Christ Jesus. [15] So where is your blessing now? For I testify that, had it been possible, you would have torn out your eyes and given them to me. [16] So have I now become your enemy by telling you the truth? [17] They zealously court you, but not commendably; for they want to exclude you, so that you may zealously court them. [18] It is good to be courted zealously to good purpose at all times, and not only when I am present with you. [19] My children, for whom I am again in the pain of childbirth until Christ is formed in you! [20] I wish I were present with you now and could change my tone, for I am perplexed about you.

Paul's Personal Plea

If Paul's rational arguments are not turning the Galatians from their folly, maybe recalling his personal affection for them will. He mentions an unspecified illness he underwent while visiting the Galatians the first time. There is nothing specific to tie this illness to Paul's famous thorn in the flesh (2 Cor 12:7), so the many scholarly suggestions about the illness are pure speculation. Some see the veiled reference to "eyes" in verse 15 as a hint that Paul may have suffered from some eye malady for a time, but this is not clear.

More important is Paul's recollection of his relationship with the Galatians. Unlike others who apparently mistreated Paul (see 2 Cor 12:7–10), he remembers that the Galatians treated him with kindness and helped him precisely when he needed assistance. He affectionately reminds them of their kind actions (v. 15, *makarismos*, lit. "blessedness," NABRE) toward him. Now he wonders where their kindness has gone. They seem willing to follow his adversaries down a false path. Even more heartrending is Paul's question: "So have I now become your enemy by telling you the truth?" This recalls many a situation in families or in communities where telling the truth wins not approval but censure. (Recall the truthful messengers throughout history who have been sacrificed when they reported the truth a ruler did not want to hear.) Paul wonders whether this is not the situation here with the Galatians. Has his defense of the truth earned him only their enmity? He admits, of course, that the Galatians must have been flattered by the agitators "courting" them. Who does not like to be courted, to be the target of winning someone's friendship? But Paul points out that the agitators' attempts at persuasion are not "commendable." Their attempts to win their loyalty are also a direct attempt to take them away from Paul's orbit so that they will become attached to the agitators.[15] In other words, they are being disingenuous.

Finally (vv. 19–20), calling the Galatians tenderly his "little children" (*tekna*),[16] he compares himself to a mother giving birth (see 1 Thess 2:7), hoping that Christ will be fully formed in them. Yet in exasperation, he admits that he is still "perplexed" about them.

AN ALLEGORY ON CHRISTIAN FREEDOM (4:21–31)

[21] Tell me, you who desire to be under the law, do you not understand the law? [22] For it is written that Abraham had two sons, one by a slave woman and the other by a free woman. [23] One, the child of the slave, was born according to the flesh; the other, the child of the free woman, was born through a promise. [24] Now this is an allegory, for these women are two covenants. One, who is Hagar, is from Mount Sinai, bearing children for slavery. [25] Now Hagar is Mount Sinai in Arabia and corresponds to the present Jerusalem, for she is a slave with her children. [26] But the other woman corresponds to the Jerusalem above; she is free, and she is our mother. [27] For it is written, "Rejoice, you barren woman, who does not give birth, burst into song and shout, you who endure no birth pangs; for the children of the desolate woman are more numerous than the children of the one who has a husband." [28] Now you, my brothers and sisters, are children of a promise, just like Isaac. [29] But just as at that time the child who was born according to the flesh persecuted the child who was born according to the Spirit, so it is now also. [30] But what does the scripture say? "Drive out the slave woman and her child; for the child of the slave woman will not

share the inheritance with the child of the free woman." [31] So then, brothers and sisters, we are children, not of the slave but of the free woman.

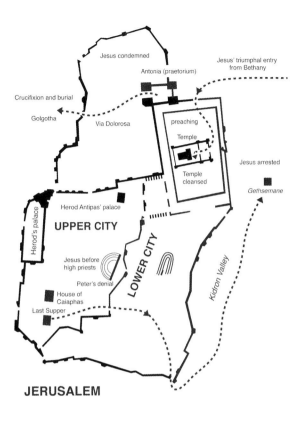

First-century Jerusalem

Madaba Map of Jerusalem

Christian Freedom

After his personal appeal, Paul specifically targets those who seemingly want to turn to the law, asking them if they really *understand* it. He turns to a second scriptural argument, offering an extended allegory (v. 24, *allēgoroumena*) on Abraham's two sons by different wives. This is one of the most perplexing passages in Galatians, especially because of Paul's convoluted application of some OT images from Genesis (see Gen 16:15; 21:2; 17:16). His argumentation is rhetorically complex and ingenious. (Consult "Paul's Allegory in Galatians 4:21–31," which attempts to diagram Paul's argument in a visual way.) Essentially, he sees two distinct lineages flowing from the same patriarch: one is the slave line (Hagar/Ishmael); the other, the freeborn (Sarah/Isaac). Note the table "Abraham and His Two Sons" for an outline of Paul's argument.[17]

Abraham and His Two Sons	
slave woman	free woman
Hagar	[Sarah, not named]
[Ishmael, not named]	Isaac
naturally born	child of promise
Mt. Sinai (!)	--------
covenant (of law)	covenant (of promise)
present Jerusalem	Jerusalem above
slave mother	our mother
child of flesh	child of Spirit

Several details in the passage are troubling. First, even if the basic contrast is clear, there are some gaps in Paul's argument. Why leave out some key names and not others? Second, there is no obvious connection in the OT between Hagar and Sinai. Hagar and Ishmael are not tied to the giving of the law to Moses, and Paul must bend the Genesis story dramatically to arrive at his analogy. Third, Paul is not clear whether his contrasts, of the two covenants, and of the present Jerusalem and "Jerusalem above" (an apocalyptic image), are intended to describe Judaism and Christianity or two types of Christians, one law observant and the other not. Scholars are divided on this last point, but it is more likely that Paul is contrasting the covenant of the law with that of the promise (de Boer, 296; Dunn, 249; Matera, 173–74), not old/new covenant (see 1 Cor 11:25; 2 Cor 3:6).[18]

Explanation of the Following Diagram

Paul's argumentation can often be convoluted, especially when he uses scriptural passages to defend his interpretation or to propose an explanation. This diagram is an attempt to visualize the flow of Paul's complex argumentation in this intriguing passage. By "allegorizing" the passage, Paul is indicating that the literal meaning of the biblical texts he cites is not the most important aspect. Rather he employs the Scriptures—and thereby the authority with which they are invested—as leading to his logical conclusion.

The parallels are clear enough, as indicated in the table "Slavery versus Freedom" below (p. 88). He begins with what the Galatians already know. Abraham had two sons by two different women, one by the slave concubine (a secondary wife) and the other by the "free" woman. They are symbolic of two covenants with two different destinies, further symbolized by the earthly Jerusalem and the Jerusalem "above." Essential to the contrast is that slavery and freedom are opposed. This is exactly the dilemma the Galatians face, for if they succumb to circumcision, they will be embracing slavery and thus abandoning the freedom that has been theirs from baptism into the Lord Jesus.

After this allegorical setup, the first scriptural citation arrives, from Isaiah 54:1 (LXX), which points to the joy of the children who come from the "mother" above because they are born of the spirit. Paul creatively applies this text to the Galatians ("you" pl.) who, like Isaac, are children of the free woman. As in the OT story, interpreted more negatively by Paul than the original text would warrant, he says the free child is "persecuted" by the slave child. (The OT text of the relation between Ishmael and Isaac only indicates that the former was playing with or perhaps teasing the latter.) This leads to the next and most important OT citation, in answer to Paul's rhetorical question about what Scripture says. This text delivers the punchline: drive out both the slave woman and her slave child because they are incompatible with the free woman and the free child (Gen 21:10). Paul concludes with a strong "therefore" that includes himself as well as the Galatians. We—that is, all who have received the Spirit and are thus free—are children from the line of freedom, not slavery.

The entire argument moves along at a dizzying pace, with some jumps over some unspoken thoughts, as indicated in the diagram. Paul's actualizing of Scripture in this instance, however, illustrates his powerful capacity to use the Scriptures to his own benefit and to reinforce his argument with scriptural authority. It likely was a direct afront to the agitators from Jerusalem (the earthly one, to be sure) who were causing such anxiety among the Galatian converts.

Paul's Allegory in Galatians 4:21–31—"it is written..."

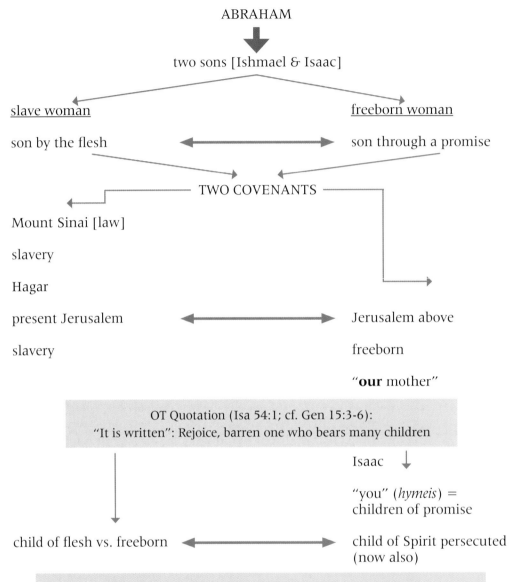

ABRAHAM

two sons [Ishmael & Isaac]

slave woman   freeborn woman

son by the flesh   son through a promise

TWO COVENANTS

Mount Sinai [law]

slavery

Hagar

present Jerusalem   Jerusalem above

slavery   freeborn

"**our** mother"

OT Quotation (Isa 54:1; cf. Gen 15:3-6):
"It is written": Rejoice, barren one who bears many children

Isaac

"you" (*hymeis*) = children of promise

child of flesh vs. freeborn   child of Spirit persecuted (now also)

OT Quotation (Gen 21:10): "What does the scripture say?
Drive out the slave woman and her child! For the child of the slave woman
shall not share the inheritance with the child of the freeborn."

"Therefore [*dio*], **we** are children not of the slavewoman but of the freeborn woman."

The Heavenly Jerusalem and Liturgy

The Second Vatican Council, in its Constitution on the Sacred Liturgy, connects the earthly experience of liturgy with our anticipation of the heavenly Jerusalem to which Paul alludes in Galatians (4:26) and which is elaborated in the Book of Revelation (21:2, 10, 22):

> In the earthly liturgy we take part in a foretaste of that heavenly liturgy which is celebrated in the holy city of Jerusalem toward which we journey as pilgrims, where Christ is sitting at the right hand of God, a minister of the holies and of the true tabernacle (see Rev 21:2; Col 3:1; Heb 8:2); we sing a hymn to the Lord's glory with all the warriors of the heavenly army; venerating the memory of the saints, we hope for some part and fellowship with them; we eagerly await the Savior, our Lord Jesus Christ, until he, our life, shall appear and we too will appear with him in glory (see Phil 3:20; Col 3:4). (*Sacrosanctum Concilium* 8)

If Paul's allegorical argumentation is not crystal clear, keep in mind that he is not only countering the agitators' arguments using the same OT passages they used to seduce the Galatians into reverting to circumcision, but he is also dictating his letter. It is easy to get lost in some of the details when one is orally summarizing one's thought. Essentially, Paul turns their interpretation of the Scriptures on its head to show that *they* are the ones who have distorted the patriarchal history in Genesis. Moreover, his contrast between the two Jerusalems is not unique to Paul. It can be found in late Jewish apocalyptic writings (4 Esd 7:26–31; 2 Bar 4:1–7) as well as later apocalyptic Christian literature (Rev 21:2, 10). In addition, the passage he cites from Isaiah 54 concerns God's promise of restoration after the exile, so it generally fits Paul's context well. He uses this passage as an aid to interpret his outlook. His argument is not about a "new" covenant but the correct way of living out the covenant of promise that comes through Abraham's true heir, Isaac. The community, now gathered in Christ, the Church, is the authentic inheritor of the free lineage. He uses the vocabulary of "child" (four

Abraham Dismissing Hagar and Ishmael by Nicolaes Maes (1653 CE)

times in the passage), along with his own parental relationship with the Galatians, to show that they are called to freedom and not to slavery. They are free children, not slaves. They are of the "Spirit" and not of the "flesh."

Slavery and Freedom

In Galatians 4–5, Paul contrasts the notions of *slavery* and *freedom* as natural consequences of the salvific actions of Jesus Christ. Paradoxically, those who voluntarily make themselves "slaves" of Christ experience the greatest freedom of all (see 1 Cor 7:22).

Slavery versus Freedom	
SLAVERY	**FREEDOM**
To the law (torah)	To live for Jesus Christ
To circumcision, the mark of identity	To live the law of love, a new identity
Symbolized by Hagar, the slave woman and Ishmael, her offspring, a "child of the flesh"	Symbolized by Sarah, the free woman, and Isaac, her offspring, a "child of the spirit"
Natural "heir"	Adopted "heirs"
Tied to the earthly Jerusalem	Tied to the Jerusalem "above"
Sealed in the covenant on Sinai	Sealed in the "new covenant" in Christ
Leads to sin	Leads to all the effects of salvation
Leads to death	Leads to eternal life

By using two quotations (Isa 54:1; Gen 21:10) as well as several other allusions from the OT and implying the slavery of the Mosaic law (Sinai), Paul develops this contrast and arrives at his dramatic conclusion (vv. 30–31). He says explicitly, "Drive out the slave woman and her son," making this a not-so-subtle demand for the Galatians to drive out the agitators from their midst. Then he caps his argument: "So then, brothers and sisters" (*adelphoi*), "we are children, not of the slave but of the free woman."

If it is true that Paul plays rather loosely with the OT passages here—a practice found also among the rabbis of his day—his main point was surely not lost on the Galatians. The unifying image of the child and heir brings home his point. In Christ, they have become adopted children, not slaves. Offering them a cultural argument, a heartfelt personal appeal, and a scriptural allegory was a powerful combination to appeal to their sensitivities. For all later generations of Christians, we see the strength of Paul's argument not to fall victim to nomism (merely being law observant) but to embrace the larger freedom we have inherited through Christ.

With this argument set forth, Paul turns to an extended exposition of true Christian freedom, the focus for the rest of the letter.

PASTORAL AND SPIRITUAL OBSERVATIONS (4:1-31)

Paul continues his argumentation in this section using reflections from familiar practices of his day, Christian tradition, a personal experience, and another example from Scripture focusing on Abraham. The example from daily life is the contrast between an heir and a slave. Who would voluntarily want to be a slave when you are the rightful heir? Paul reminds the Galatians that they were, in fact, "slaves" to certain pagan practices, but in Christ, all that has changed. They should thereby not seek another form of slavery! We can ask if we, too, are not still "enslaved" by forces that we permit to control our lives. One can think of addictions, surely—alcohol, sex, money, gambling, power, influence, lying, the Internet, and so on—but there are many bad habits and peccadillos that also infringe on our true Christian freedom. We may not be subject to "elemental spirits," but we do indeed have our modern means of enslavement.

Regarding Christian tradition, Paul subtly recalls the incarnation (4:4), the gracious action of God that set the history of salvation in motion, and a liturgical ritual that recalls Jesus's manner of prayer (4:6; see Matt 6:9). The ability to pray to God in intimate fashion—*Abba*! Father!—is a hallmark of Christian identity. In a sense, it once more recalls our baptism, wherein we became children of God. To pray in this manner is to respect this identity that God has freely bestowed upon us, giving us a unique dignity.

In this passage, we also get another glimpse of Paul's personal life—a reminder that our own personal experiences form an essential part of our own lives. In this case, Paul recalls some unspecified illness when he was present to the Galatians (4:13). They responded, as would any decent concerned individuals, by caring for him. Apparently, the care was very tender and helpful, for he affirms that they received him as if he were "an angel of God, like Christ Jesus" (4:14). This is not faint praise. It is also, of course, the way members of the family of God should act toward one another. Treating every person as a fellow human being is essential because each person represents "another Christ." Recall the parable of the sheep and goats (Matt 25:31–46), when both sets of characters did not realize that in aiding or ignoring the stranger—the naked, the hungry and thirsty, the imprisoned—they were aiding or ignoring Christ. Notice that Paul is not threatening the Galatians with punishment here. No, he is trying to appeal to their better nature to return to the right path and to resist the attempts to detour them from authentic faith. Paul's true love and appreciation for the Galatians comes through in this passage. He compares himself to a woman in labor on their behalf (4:19)! No wonder he is disappointed in them. When family members (or parishioners) really go astray, it is very hurtful. It feels like a betrayal, which is exactly the feeling that Paul hints at in this letter.

Finally, Paul offers another scriptural support. We cannot overestimate his reliance upon the Scriptures for undergirding his message. He uses the allegory of Abraham's two wives and their respective children to demonstrate that there are only two paths. One can choose the path of slavery or the path of freedom. Which will it be? Which will you choose? How often Paul returns to the Scriptures to further his message. His familiarity with the Scriptures is admirable, and in this case his notion of the two paths is reminiscent of a prominent OT teaching found in the Deuteronomic and wisdom traditions. In Deuteronomy, Moses famously sets forth the two choices for the people of Israel. While describing God's commands, he says, "I call heaven and earth to witness against you today that I have set before you life and death, blessings and curses. Choose life so that you and your descendants may live" (Deut 30:19 NRSV).

The Wisdom tradition also emphasizes the choice that people have in how to live their lives. Consider Psalm 1, the wisdom Psalm at the very head of the Psalter (1:1–6). It describes the path of the righteous who live in accordance with God's commands. They will flourish like trees next to streams of water. The wicked, however, will be thwarted; they will be like chaff thrown to the wind.

In a sense, Paul offers the Galatians a similar choice, but with one major difference. Their choice is not based on obedience to the law but rather upon accepting the redemption and salvation achieved by the cross of Christ and now freely offered to them as God's children. They no longer need to worry about the law, but they must embrace the life of faith. If they choose slavery, they will lose their inheritance. If they choose to remain "heirs," they will receive the promise of Abraham.

Note that true freedom remains in view. God does not force salvation down anyone's throat, but the offer is always there. Once set on the path to the new creation, why would anyone refuse?

REFLECTION QUESTIONS

1. How does Paul contrast "slave" and "child" in this section of the letter? Does the contrast still apply even in a society where literal slavery is now forbidden (though other forms of slavery still exist!)?
2. Metaphorically, people can be "slaves" to all sorts of realities. What kinds of "enslavement" are particularly seductive today? What can people do to obtain true "freedom" from such enslavement?
3. Are you surprised that Paul sometimes presents himself as a "mother" concerned for her children (Gal 4:19)? How do you interpret such metaphorical language? How well would it have been accepted in a patriarchally oriented society that was so characteristic of Paul's world?

4. How effective would Paul's contrast of the two women and their children have been for the Galatians? How well did you follow Paul's development of thought? What are the holes in his arguments, and do they make any difference?
5. Explain the contrast of the two "Jerusalems" in this section. Why is Jerusalem at the heart of Paul's argument? How does Jerusalem relate to Mount Sinai, which Paul also invokes?

5
EXHORTATION TO CHRISTIAN LIVING (5:1–6:10)

Having concluded his second scriptural argument—the extended allegory about true heirs—Paul begins an extensive ethical exhortation, technically called paraenesis. This, however, is not merely a generic moral exhortation. It flows from Paul's argument in the letter thus far and constitutes a clarion call to the Galatians to implement the new life of faith they have received in baptism with ethical uprightness worthy of the call. This section elaborates the freedom that Christ has brought the Galatians, which they are in danger of throwing away. One can discern four main divisions in this section of the body:

Initial Exhortations on Faith and Freedom (5:1–6)

A Further Plea to the Galatians (5:7–12)

A Call to Freedom for Service and the Contrast between Flesh and Spirit (5:13–26)

An Exhortation on Life in the Community of Christ (6:1–10)

INITIAL EXHORTATIONS ON FAITH AND FREEDOM (5:1-6)

5 ¹ For freedom Christ has set us free. Stand firm, therefore, and do not submit again to a yoke of slavery. ² Look! I, Paul, am telling you that if you let yourselves be circumcised, Christ will be of no benefit to you. ³ Once again I testify to every man who lets himself be circumcised that he is obliged to keep the entire law. ⁴ You who want to be justified by the law have cut yourselves off from Christ; you have fallen away from grace. ⁵ For through the Spirit, by faith, we eagerly wait for the hope of righteousness. ⁶ For in Christ Jesus neither circumcision nor uncircumcision counts for anything; the only thing that counts is faith working through love.

The first division of the exhortation (vv. 1–6) strongly reminds the Galatians of the freedom that Christ has achieved for them and its stark contrast to the "yoke [burden] of slavery" that they are in danger of taking up. Paul, emphatically ("Now, I Paul…"), mentions the specific issue of circumcision, which has been implicit in the letter from the beginning. The temptation to accept circumcision and all it implies is the precipitating cause of the problem in Galatia. He warns them that "Christ will be no benefit to you" if they seek that enslavement.

The first verse functions like a hinge. Some interpreters see it as concluding the previous section, despite the lack of a connecting particle. It is a fitting conclusion to the preceding allegory, but it also introduces the exhortation using both the noun and verb for "freedom" (the root *eleuther-*). Therefore, we see it here as the beginning of the paraenetic section by using the notion of freedom.[1] Since Christ has freed us (from slavery) for freedom, a truth he had already emphasized (2:4), now Paul strongly exhorts them, "Stand firm!" He then shifts to the first-person emphatic form to highlight his message ("Listen! I, Paul"). He is testifying to the truth of the gospel message. He knows that for those in Christ, circumcision amounts to nothing and only ties them to the obligations of the law. In fact, as he states, it leads to separation from Christ and a fall from grace (v. 4).[2]

Faith and Love

Pope Benedict XVI (Joseph Ratzinger, b. 1927) was a theologian before becoming pope. As pope, he applied his theological training to many of his teachings. In one of his encyclicals (formal teaching letters), he picks up profoundly on Paul's connection between faith and love, noting that love involved more than doing charitable actions:

Those who work for the Church's charitable organizations must be distinguished by the fact that they do not merely meet the needs of the moment, but they dedicate themselves to others with heartfelt concern, enabling them to experience the richness of their humanity. Consequently, in addition to their necessary professional training, these charity workers need a "formation of the heart": they need to be led to that encounter with God in Christ which awakens their love and opens their spirits to others. As a result, love of neighbor will no longer be for them a commandment imposed, so to speak, from without, but a consequence deriving from their faith, a faith which becomes active through love (cf. Gal 5:6). *Deus Caritas Est* ("God Is Love," 2005), 31a.

The expression "faith working through love" can be interpreted in several ways. It could mean "faith expressing itself through love" or perhaps faith being "energized by love." Most important is the connection it affirms between faith and love. Faith is not merely empty words; it is not opposed to actions. Throughout his paraenesis, Paul emphasizes love concretely as the way Christians show that they are truly free in Christ. Neither circumcision nor uncircumcision matters. What really matters is putting faith in action. By faith and through the Spirit, Paul also says, "We eagerly await the hope of righteousness" (v. 5). This is part of Paul's eschatological outlook, viewing the end time of the coming of God's kingdom, when true righteousness will reign. Paul likely here means not the hope that comes from righteousness (upright, ethical living) but the righteousness (the gift freely given of being made right) that comes from God alone.

James and Paul

In the history of interpretation, especially since the time of the Reformation, interpreters have debated the relationship between faith and works. This has often been characterized as the opposition between Paul, as expressed especially in Galatians and Romans, and James, who seemingly takes another view in his letter.

In James, we read, "What good is it, my brothers and sisters, if you say you have faith but do not have works? Can faith save you? If a brother or sister is naked and lacks daily food, and one of you says to them, 'Go in peace; keep warm and eat your fill,' and yet you do not supply their bodily needs, what is the good of that? So faith by itself, if it has no works, is dead. But someone will say, 'You have faith and I have works.' Show me your faith apart from your works, and I by my works will show you my faith" (Jas 2:14–18 NRSV).

Some see in this passage an anti-Pauline message. A careful reading of Paul and James indicates that the faith/good works contrast is a false dichotomy. Especially here in Galatians 5, Paul shows that good works—that is, living one's life according to the supreme commandment of love—is not opposed to faith but a way of implementing one's faith. So, one need not choose between Paul or James. Both are in the NT and both offer a consistent view that faith and love, faith and good works, go hand in hand.

A FURTHER PLEA TO THE GALATIANS (5:7–12)

[7] You were running well; who hindered you from obeying the truth? [8] Such persuasion does not come from the one who calls you. [9] A little yeast leavens the whole batch of dough. [10] I am confident about you in the Lord that you will not think otherwise. But whoever is confusing you will pay the penalty. [11] Now, brothers and sisters, if I am still preaching circumcision, why am I still being persecuted? In that case the stumbling block of the cross has been removed. [12] I wish those who are disturbing you would also castrate themselves!

---

1 Cor 1:23; 5:6; 8:9; 9:24–26; Rom 6:18; Phil 2:16; 3:14; 1 Pet 2:16

The second division (vv. 7–12) shifts now to a further personal plea on Paul's part, but he immediately draws the Galatians into the conversation with an affirmation and a question. He will then conclude with biting sarcasm.

Using the athletic image of a footrace he had also earlier used of himself (2:2), he says affirmatively, "You were running well." (As pointed out earlier, such athletic imagery is present elsewhere in Paul and was familiar throughout the Greco-Roman world where athletics were admired; e.g., 1 Cor 9:24–27; Phil 2:16; 2:14). In other words, you were on the right path; you were doing well in the life of faith. Then the question: "Who hindered you from obeying the truth?"[3] The referent of the singular "who" is not clear. Is it generic, almost in a rhetorical way, or does Paul have someone among the agitators in mind (see also the singular in 3:1; 5:10b)? It may refer to their leader whom Paul has mentioned elsewhere (2:4). In any case, Paul sees that their attempt at "persuasion" has corrupted the Galatians, like leaven permeates a whole batch of dough. (Leaven or yeast in the Bible is normally a negative image, likely because a small amount mysteriously affects a whole batch; 1 Cor 5:6–7; Mark 8:15.)

During this challenging assessment, Paul briefly affirms the Galatians again, first by saying he is confident "you will take no other view than mine," and then addressing them once more as "brothers and sisters" (vv. 10–11). In this section, Paul makes a play on words that is difficult to appreciate in English, using words with the same root that mean "confident," "persuaded," and "persuasion" (forms of *peith*, vv. 7–10), which gives his argument more rhetorical force. He also says "whoever" (singular, perhaps implying the leader of the agitators) is causing the problem will "pay the penalty." His question about why *he* is being persecuted may at first seem awkward, but it implies that Paul, ironically, has been accused (probably by the opponents) of still (*eti*) preaching circumcision. For Paul, this is a patently absurd charge. The Galatians know well that, as apostle to the gentiles, Paul regarded circumcision no longer applicable for those among the gentiles who came to faith in Christ.

As he had warned against the corruption of the gospel earlier in the letter (2:6–9), here he asserts that such a charge would remove "the stumbling block of the cross" (*skandalon*; see also 1 Cor 1:23). In other words, it would lead to a false faith, an easy path rather than the more challenging one that comes from the gospel message that Paul preached.

Finally, Paul ends with a sarcastic wish. In exasperation, he concludes by wishing that those (plural) who are disturbing (NJB, "unsettling"; NABRE, "upsetting") the Galatians by promoting circumcision would go all the way, castrating themselves (RSV, "mutilate"; NIV, "emasculate")! This startling image makes sense, perhaps, in the Greco-Roman world, where the Jewish practice of circumcision was equated with mutilation of the body. (According to Deut 23:1–2 LXX, men whose genitals were removed were excluded from the assembly.) For the Greeks and Romans, the Jewish practice of circumcision was a barbaric practice, equivalent to mutilating unnaturally the human body. Additionally, adult males in the Greco-Roman world would not have looked forward to circumcision, which is why some who were attracted to Judaism's ethical teachings nonetheless refused to convert fully to Judaism and remained "God-fearers" (see Acts 10:22; 13:16, 26).[4] This may be a strong way for Paul to end his personal appeal, but he makes his point boldly. It is not intended literally but expresses with hyperbole Paul's exasperation; it must have turned heads when they heard it.

Augustine on the Image in Galatians 5:12

Saint Augustine creatively interprets this strong sentiment on Paul's part as "a blessing under the appearance of a curse," namely, Paul desiring that the Galatians would "become eunuchs for the sake of the kingdom of heaven, and cease to sow carnal seed" (Plumer, 203; see Matt 19:12).

A CALL TO FREEDOM FOR SERVICE AND THE CONTRAST BETWEEN FLESH AND SPIRIT (5:13–26)

[13] For you were called to freedom, brothers and sisters; only do not use your freedom as an opportunity for the flesh, but through love become servants to one another. [14] For the whole law is summed up in one commandment, namely, "You shall love your neighbor as yourself." [15] If, however, you bite and devour one another, watch out that you are not consumed by one another!

[16] But I say, live by the Spirit, and do not gratify the desires of the flesh. [17] For what the flesh desires is opposed to the Spirit, and what the Spirit desires is opposed to the flesh; for these are opposed to each other, to prevent you from doing what you want. [18] But if you are led by the Spirit, you are not under the law.

¹⁹ Now the works of the flesh are obvious: sexual immorality, impurity, licentiousness, ²⁰ idolatry, sorcery, enmities, strife, jealousy, anger, quarrels, dissensions, factions, ²¹ envy, drunkenness, carousing, and things like these. I am warning you, as I warned you before: those who do such things will not inherit the kingdom of God. ²² By contrast, the fruit of the Spirit is love, joy, peace, patience, kindness, generosity, faithfulness, ²³ humility, and self-control. There is no law against such things. ²⁴ And those who belong to Christ Jesus have crucified the flesh with its passions and desires. ²⁵ If we live by the Spirit, let us also walk in line with the Spirit. ²⁶ Let us not become conceited, provoking one another, envying one another.

Lev 19:18
Matt 22:39 // Luke 10:27; Rom 13:8–10; 1 Cor 13:1–13
Rom 1:29–31; 7:22–24; Phil 2:3; Col 2:8; 3:5–10;
  1 Tim 1:9–10; Rev 22:15
Rom 8:5; 1 Cor 13:4–7; 2 Cor 6:6; Eph 5:9; Phil 2:3;
  Col 2:8; 3:5–10; 1 Tim 1:4,12; 2 Pet 1:5–7

In this section, Paul returns to the heart of his ethical message—the freedom that has been the focus of much of the body of the letter—and expanding on what it means concretely, especially in the contrast between flesh and Spirit that is a prominent theme in Paul's theology. There are two parts. The first (vv. 13–15) is a general reminder of freedom, coupled with a warning if they do not see how it is to be lived from the perspective of love. The second and lengthier section (vv. 16–26) describes freedom through the contrast between flesh and Spirit. Each path involves ethical choices that would have been familiar to the Galatians in their Greco-Roman culture.

Pope Benedict XVI

Pope Benedict XVI (Joseph Ratzinger, b. 1927), who surprised the Church and the world by resigning as supreme pontiff of the Catholic Church on February 28, 2013, has left the Church a rich legacy of theological writings, many of them strongly influenced by Sacred Scripture. In one of his published letters, he used an example from Galatians that shows how this section of Paul's letter can be applied to a modern situation. The context was his explanation to the bishops for why he had removed the excommunication of four bishops of the Saint Pius X Society ordained by Archbishop Marcel Lefebvre in 1988:

During the days when I first had the idea of writing this letter, by chance, during a visit to the Roman Seminary, I had to interpret and comment on Galatians 5:13-15. I was surprised at the directness with which that passage speaks to us about the present moment: "Do not use your freedom as an opportunity for the flesh, but through love be servants of one another. For the whole law is fulfilled in one word: 'You shall love your neighbor as yourself.' But if you bite and devour one another, take heed that you are not consumed by one another." I am always tempted to see these words as another of the rhetorical excesses which we occasionally find in Saint Paul. To some extent that may also be the case. But sad to say, this "biting and devouring" also exists in the Church today, as expression of a poorly understood freedom. Should we be surprised that we too are no better than the Galatians? That at the very least we are threatened by the same temptations? That we must always learn anew the proper use of freedom? And that we must always learn anew the supreme priority, which is love? (Pope Benedict XVI, "Letter to the Bishops of the Catholic Church," March 10, 2009)

Paul begins with an emphatic "For *you* were called to freedom, brothers and sisters" (v. 13). Freedom, Paul knows, can be defined in different ways. Some see freedom as living totally without constraints. In an American context, it often means not being constrained by government interference. It can also mean unbridled, selfish, self-centered, self-promoting behavior. Even worse, Paul sees the danger that the Galatians will abuse one another because of their freedom (v. 15). This is not, however, the Christian notion of freedom. Paul immediately ties freedom to love, as he did earlier (v. 6). In fact, Paul quotes a part of the OT law (Lev 18:19) that Jesus had made the centerpiece of his own ethical teaching: "For the whole law is fulfilled in one statement, namely, 'You shall love your neighbor as yourself'" (v. 14; see Matt 22:39; Rom 13:8–10). This is one of the rare instances in the Pauline letters where Paul alludes to or cites the ethical teaching of Jesus. Note also that it includes a positive use of the word *law* as it pertains to the Mosaic law. Love trumps all the law, and living in love is to live ultimately as a free individual. This type of freedom is embodied by service to one another rather than by exercising "fleshly" human desires. Freedom, for Paul, is thus not only freedom *from* but freedom *for*. The type of service he envisions is not simply ministry to one another (*diakoneō*) but becoming servants (slaves) of one another (*douleuete*). Paul is being forceful in calling the Galatians to humble service of one another. This is the core of the freedom they have received in Christ. One Catholic commentator, the late Cardinal Carlo Maria Martini (1927–2012), who was known for his pastoral approach to the Bible, wrote of Paul's attitude,

Paul's liberty of spirit is amazing: he owes nothing to anyone but Christ; through him, therefore, he owes it to everyone. He need please no one and respond to no one but Christ and the community knows very well that he is not there to please, to make people happy and to fulfill their expectations but he is there to serve Christ. (Martini, 53)

Such is the connection between freedom and service.

Paul then explains his instruction very concretely by contrasting life in the Spirit with life in the flesh, beginning with the latter. These two positions are strictly opposed: you cannot live in the Spirit and remain tied to the law; you cannot remain neutral but must choose. Employing a technique of ethical choices to be avoided, which was a commonplace practice in Paul's world, especially among various philosophical schools like the Stoics, Paul offers an extensive list of fifteen "works of the flesh" (vv. 19–21), concluding with a general "and things like these." We should note that for Paul, "flesh" (*sarx*) does not always have the connotation of sexuality that modern American English tends to associate with it. Rather, it is a general term for all that is finite, limited, and evil in the world, although it also includes sexual sins.

How We Need to Behave

Jean-Jacques Olier, founder of the Sulpicians and a leader in the seventeenth-century French school of spirituality, was enamored of the letters of Paul. In one of Olier's own letters he invokes a set of images that help to explain the essence of Paul's message in Galatians 5, even though there is no explicit citation of the passage. Olier creatively combines the image of a child, the Spirit, and right conduct as follows:

> Being a child in this way has nothing to do with human prudence and wisdom but to go where obedience and the movement of the Holy Spirit carries one. A child goes with returning to wherever he is led, and the children of God go wherever God's Spirit leads them. They do not worry that what they do is according to the laws of this world or if it conforms to its customs. Rather, they are content with the wisdom of faith, which is itself God's wisdom, which he gives to his children as a rule and for light. They abandon themselves purely without second thought to this holy conduct....
>
> So this is the kind of conduct the children of God possess by his divine Spirit, who, children though they are, have a wisdom a thousand times more solid, more demanding, and more regulated than the whole world combined. (Jean-Jacques Olier [1608-57], *Lettres Spirituelles* vol. 1 [Paris: Gaumé, 1831], 148 [au. trans.].)

If the list of vices is not exhaustive, it is colorful. It encompasses many of the evils one sees in humanity, from sexual depravity to jealousy, envy, drunkenness, and all kinds of self-ish and self-destructive behavior, both individual and relational. The list begins with sexual sins that the Jews often alleged were characteristic of the Greco-Roman world and that they found abhorrent, but it includes many examples of "bad behavior." Most of the terms occur elsewhere in Paul's letters.[5] It is not a matter of going from bad to worse or vice versa. Rather, living in the flesh (i.e., in a strictly human, finite fashion) leads one down a path of self-serving and evil attitudes and actions that ultimately divide human beings. Living in the flesh harms community. Paul sternly warns that those who engage in such practices "will not inherit the kingdom," which is tantamount to saying that they will throw away their rightful heritage as "children of God" if they do such things. Note that Paul includes an explicit warning that, if they engage in such anti-Spirit behavior, the Galatians may not "inherit the kingdom of God" (v. 21). This is one of the rare occurrences of the expression "kingdom of God" in Paul's letters (see Rom 14:17; 1 Cor 4:20; 15:50; Col 4:11).[6] It possibly has an apocalyptic background in the belief that one day, the day of judgment, there will be a divine accounting for human behavior (cf. also 6:8).

By contrast, Paul immediately lists "the fruit of the Spirit" (vv. 22–23). The singular "fruit" (*karpos*) is noteworthy. Life in the Spirit is not simply a matter of "works" or indi-vidual demands of the law. The Spirit singularly leads to upright traits. Life in the Spirit is lived in an entirely new key (see Rom 8:1–17). Whereas fleshly living comprises individ-ualistic behaviors that negatively impact communal relationships, life in the Spirit pro-duces a singular "fruit" that generates attitudes and actions that are considerate of others. Some scholars see in the list three groups of three (Matera, 209; Martyn, 498–99), whether through thematic relationships or artistic style, but this is not certain. In comparison to the list of vices, it is significant that the first virtue on this second list is love. Since Paul has made such a point of the law of love above (v. 14; see also 6:2 "law of Christ"), perhaps he is drawing attention to it here in first place, leading down to the final virtue mentioned, self-control (*egkrateia*). This latter was a prized virtue among some Greek philosophers and perhaps could have also resonated with the Galatians. Ingeniously, Paul uses the language of crucifixion regarding the removal of the temptations of the flesh. Those who are in Christ or who belong to him (lit. "of Christ") "have crucified the flesh" with all its passions and desires. Using a balanced chiasm (parallel a-b-b'-a' format in Greek), Paul says, "If we live by the Spirit, let us also walk in line with the Spirit," that is, be guided by the Spirit. ("Walking" is a biblical metaphor for ethical conduct in life; e.g., Deut 5:33; Prov 8:20; Mark 7:5.)[7] By including himself here ("we"), he emphasizes a universal faith. It obligates *all* believers. He reinforces his conviction by a final reminder not to be conceited, not to pro-voke one another, and not to be envious of one another.

"Against Such There Is No Law"

John Calvin sees in the expression "against such there is no law" (Gal 5:23b) a deeper meaning than simply a teaching directed against good works. He explains,

> Some understand these words as meaning simply that the law is not directed against good works, "from evil manners have sprung good laws." But Paul's real meaning is deeper and less obvious; namely, that, where the Spirit reigns, the law has no longer any dominion. By molding our hearts to his own righteousness, the Lord delivers us from the severity of the law, so that our intercourse with himself is not regulated by its covenant, nor our consciences bound by its sentence of condemnation. (Calvin, 168)

Note also that this remarkable passage (vv. 16–26) can be structured as another, longer chiasm, as follows, introduced by a solemn declaration, "I say, then…" (v. 16a), and concluding with the exhortation not to provoke one another (v. 26), two statements that frame the actual chiasm:

a) Live by the Spirit, not by the flesh (v. 16b)

  b) The Spirit and flesh are opposed (v. 17)

    c) Be guided by the Spirit, not the law (v. 18)

     d) Illustration of the works of the flesh (v. 19–21a)

      e) Those who do such deeds will *not* inherit the kingdom of God (v. 21b)

     d′) Illustration of the fruit of the Spirit (v. 22a)

    c′) Against such, there is no law (v. 23b)

  b′) Whoever is in Christ crucifies the flesh with its passions and desires (v. 24)

a′) Live by the Spirit, follow the Spirit (v. 25)

If one accepts this parallelism (Lémonon, *Pour lire*, 91), it helps reinforce Paul's contrast between the flesh and Spirit in an artistic fashion, making the centerpiece of the chiasm the kingdom of God, which is the goal of salvation—life with God. In other words, Paul's contrast provides a stern warning to the Galatians not to abandon the path of the Spirit by seeking the works of the flesh.

AN EXHORTATION ON LIFE IN THE COMMUNITY OF CHRIST (6:1–10)

6 ¹ Brothers and sisters, even if anyone is caught in a transgression, you who are spiritual should restore such a one in a spirit of gentleness, taking care that you yourself are also not tempted. ² Bear one another's burdens, and so fulfill the law of Christ. ³ For anyone who thinks he is something, even though he is nothing, deceives himself. ⁴ Let each person examine their own work; then that work, rather than their neighbor's work, will become a cause for boasting. ⁵ For all must carry their own burden. ⁶ The one who is taught the word must share all good things with their teacher. ⁷ Do not be deceived; God is not mocked, for you reap whatever you sow. ⁸ If you sow to your own flesh, you will reap corruption from the flesh; but if you sow to the Spirit, you will reap eternal life from the Spirit. ⁹ So let us not grow weary in doing good, for we will reap at harvest time, if we do not give up. ¹⁰ So, then, whenever we have an opportunity, let us work for the good of all, and especially for those of the household of faith.

> **Matt 18:15–17; Rom 14:12; 1 Cor 3:18; 9:21; 10:12–13; 2 Cor 12:11; Col 3:13; 1 Thess 5:15; Jas 5:19–20; Heb 12:1–3**
> **Prov 11:18**
> **Rom 8:6–13; 1 Cor 9:14; 10:12–13; 16:21; 1 Thess 5:15; 2 Thess 3:13**

The fourth and final section (6:1–10) outlines the quality of life that should be characteristic of those in the Spirit, especially "those of the family of faith" (v. 10), namely the Christian household.

Reinforcing his fraternal relationship with the Galatians by calling them "brothers and sisters" again (NRSV "My friends"), Paul winds down his ethical exhortations with reminders of both individual and communal responsibilities. Note that he begins (v. 1) with a plea for "you who are spiritual" (also NABRE, RSV; NRSV "you who have received the Spirit") to restore anyone who has been in transgression, such as those he has mentioned earlier (2:17; 5:19–21). Paul shows a tender side here, despite his stern warnings elsewhere. The first response to transgression should be to try to rehabilitate "in a spirit of gentleness" the one who transgresses (cf. 2 Cor 2:5–8; Matt 18:15). He ties this appeal to the reminder to "take care that you yourselves are not tempted" (lit. "look to yourself"; cf. Phil 2:3–4, where the same verb is used).

Bearing One Another's Burdens

Marius Victorinus (ca. 283-362), who wrote the first Latin commentaries on Paul's letters, draws out the implication of Paul's passionate exhortation in Galatians 6:2 to bear one another's burdens, tying it to Christ's own sufferings, with the following explanation:

Paul has reverted to the plural address, in order that every person would bear the other people's faults, so that what one suffers, each would endure, put up with, and correct in so far as possible. For this is what it means to bear burdens: to endure patiently the weakness of another person and correct it....For Christ himself was patient in this way: he both bore our ills and put up with adversity on account of our ills. (Cooper, 337)

Then he lists a series of practical advice. It is not merely directed to the Galatian men but to all persons (*anthrōpos*). It begins with "Bear one another's burdens" (cf. 5:13; Col 3:13). Individually, Paul reminds them not to deceive themselves into thinking they really are someone, to bear their own "loads," to "test" their own work rather than their neighbor's, and to remember that you will reap what you sow. Regarding communal responsibilities, Paul reminds them that they are to carry their own burden, not to grow weary of doing what is right, not to give up, and to work for the good of *all*, emphasizing especially the family of faith. Throughout this section, Paul employs the metaphorical language of sowing and reaping, and the mention of having an "opportunity" (*kairon*; also v. 9, where the same word means "harvest time") places the teaching in an eschatological vein, pointing to the time when they will "inherit the kingdom" (5:21). He warns that "God is not mocked, for you reap whatever you sow." That does not leave much room for fudging. Our deeds ultimately have consequences. This is not because they earn us salvation; rather, they can show that we refuse to accept God's gracious hand of salvation by remaining obstinate in our sinful ways. Sowing and reaping (as well as the harvest time) are obvious agricultural metaphors here for human actions and their ramifications (see also "bearing fruit" language in Matt 3:8–10; 12:33). Note how Paul contrasts the two options: "If you sow *to your own flesh*, you will reap corruption from the flesh; but if you sow to the Spirit, you will reap eternal life from the Spirit." This is precisely what he had demonstrated in the earlier contrasting lists of vices and virtues, the former from the "flesh" and the latter from the "Spirit" (5:16–25). The words in italics, however, emphasize the individual responsibility that comes from choosing the wrong path, whereas eternal life comes "from the Spirit." Throughout this passage, Paul is exhorting the Galatians to perseverance, not giving up or losing heart, regardless of how difficult it might be to live in the Spirit.

The meaning of verse 6 may not be immediately clear to the casual reader, but the Galatians likely understood the message: "Those who are taught the word must share in all good things with their teacher." The Greek text is singular rather than plural, and the repetition of the root *katēch-* (whence our words *catechesis, catechumen, catechism*) makes the close connection between the teacher and the one who is taught. In context, one might suppose that sharing in "all good things" refers to spiritual treasures that result from proper ethical behavior. But more likely, Paul is making a subtle appeal to material goods, that is, to donations for the collection that preoccupied him for most of his missionary life (2:10; Phil 4:15; Wright, 76; Byrne, 48). This may seem "cheeky" on Paul's part with this community with which he has been so challenging. But Paul never let such considerations stand in the way of what he considered essential. However, note that in Romans 15:26, the Galatians are missing from the list of those who contributed to the collection (Macedonians and Achaians). Does this mean Paul's appeal fell on deaf ears?

Paul then concludes his ethical section with strong exhortations that leave no doubt in the Galatians' minds about what they should return to: the life they received in baptism into Christ and that now demands they live in a manner characteristic of this new identity. It is not found in the law of Moses but in the law of Christ (John 13:34; 1 Cor 9:20–21).

The Complexity of Paul's Teaching on the Law

To illustrate the complexity of Paul's teaching on the law, see the chart below, which lists tensions or even contradictions in Paul's thought. Remember, of course, that these statements are taken out of context, and therefore one cannot draw too many conclusions. Context is essential for a justifiable interpretation. At the same time, however, scholars have long noted that Paul is not entirely consistent in his thought regarding the Mosaic law. We should also note that there appears to be no distinction in Paul between the word *law* being used with or without the definite article (i.e., law/the law, e.g. in Rom 7:7-12). The topic is too complex to be treated here in detail, let alone resolved, but the information reinforces the necessity of interpreting Paul with great care. There are positive, negative, and seemingly neutral uses of the word *law* in Paul, and each passage must be considered in context with care.

REFERENCE	NEGATIVE STATEMENTS ON THE LAW	REFERENCE	POSITIVE STATEMENTS ON THE LAW
Gal 3:25	"But now that faith has come, we are no longer under a custodian [*paidogōgos*]." (i.e., the law)	Rom 7:12	"So the law is holy, and the commandment is holy and just and good."
Rom 5:20	"Law came in, to increase the trespass." (au. trans.)	Rom 7:14	"We know that the law is spiritual."
2 Cor 3:6	"For the written code kills." (au. trans.)	Rom 3:31	"Do we then overthrow the law by this faith? By no means! On the contrary, we uphold the law."
Rom 10:4	"For Christ is the end [*telos*] of the law."	Gal 3:21	"Is the law then against the promises of God? Certainly not."

Continued

Rom 3:20–21	"For no human being will be justified in his sight by works of the law, since through the law comes knowledge of sin. But now the righteousness of God has been manifested apart from the law." (au. trans.)	Rom 3:1–2	"Then what advantage has the Jew? Or what is the value of circumcision? Much, in every way!"
Gal 3:10	"For all who rely on works of the law are under a curse."	Rom 7:7	"What then should we say? That the law is sin? By no means!"
Gal 3:11	"Now it is evident that no one is justified before God by the law."	Rom 7:13	"Did that which is good, then, bring death to me? By no means! It was sin, working death in me through what is good, in order that sin might be shown to be sin, and through the commandment might become sinful beyond measure."
Rom 7:8	"Apart from the law sin lies dead." (i.e., the law keeps sin alive.)	Rom 7:22	"For I delight in the law of God in my inmost self."
Rom 7:9–10	"But when the commandment came in, sin revived and I died."		
Rom 7:10–11	"…the very commandment that promised life proved to be death to me. For sin, finding opportunity in the commandment, deceived me and by it killed me."		
Rom 3:28	"For we hold that a person is justified by faith apart from works of the law." (au. trans.)		
2 Cor 3:14–15	"For to this day, when they read the old covenant, the same veil remains unlifted, because only through Christ is it taken away. Yes, to this day whenever Moses is read a veil lies over their minds." (au. trans.)		

POSSIBLE NEUTRAL STATEMENTS IN PAUL ON THE LAW

1 Corinthians 9:20-21: "To the Jews I became as a Jew, in order to win Jews; to those under the law, I became as one under the law—though not being myself under the law—that I might win those under the law. To those outside the law I became as one outside the law—not being without law toward God but under the law of Christ—that I might win those outside the law." (This may indicate that one can for a time be law observant.)

1 Corinthians 7:17-20: In the context of everyone remaining in their state, whether circumcised or uncircumcised, Paul says, "Everyone should remain in the state in which he was called." (His may imply that the law still has some validity.)

Galatians 6:2: "Bear one another's burdens, and so fulfill the law of Christ [*ton nomon tou Christou*]." (This opens the issues of whether it is a "new" law.)

Galatians 6:15: "For neither circumcision counts for anything, nor uncircumcision, but a new creation." (This may mitigate the importance of the law, at least regarding circumcision.)

Romans 8:2: "For the law [*ho nomos*] of the Spirit of life in Christ Jesus has set you free from the law [*tou nomou*] of sin and death." (This contrasts life in the Spirit and in Christ with sin and death.)

Romans 3:27: "Then what becomes of boasting? It is excluded. By what law? By that of works? No, but by the law of faith [*dia nomou pisteōs*]". (Here is another use of the word, in relation to faith.)

Paul's use of "the law of Christ" (*ho nomos tou Christou*, v. 2) is striking. The same word for "law" is thus used of the Mosaic law and the law of Christ. Scholars are not in agreement on the precise meaning of the expression. It might well mean the love commandment as taught by Christ, which fits well with the larger paraenetic context (cf. 5:14). More recently, some suggest that it means the Mosaic law as lived out and fulfilled by Christ (Matera, 220–21). So, it is not a *new* law or an alternative to the law of Moses, but that same God-given law—which otherwise leads to a "works mentality" and sin and death, and not to salvation—concretely interpreted and lived out by Jesus Christ. The advantage of the latter interpretation is that it takes seriously the mature context of Paul's letters and the sometimes-ambiguous way Paul uses his language (cf. Rom 3:27; 8:2). Regardless, the law of Christ is indeed related to the law of love, which is how those who live in the Spirit will live their lives concretely.

PASTORAL AND SPIRITUAL OBSERVATIONS

This section of Galatians strikes a chord in most contemporary readers because we recognize specific ethical instruction that provides food for thought. It offers us an examination of conscience (6:4), if you will, on how our behavior conforms to what Paul describes as the ideal for those who live in faith. It provides a template on how to live according to the Spirit and not according to the flesh. There are five observations that come from this section.

The first concerns Paul's presentation of "freedom" as the opening exhortation. He is adamant about Christian freedom. Christ has set us free, so we should firmly resist any attempt to return to any form of slavery. Ethically, one might ask, how does freedom help us live a better Christian life? Paul's answer is that the truly free person in Christ no longer worries about conformity to one or another aspect of God's commandments. A truly free individual sets about living out the only law that counts—the law of love, which is indeed the law of Christ. This is precisely what Paul explains a few lines later, when he reminds us again of our Christian freedom and connects it to love of God and love of neighbor (5:13–15). It is not mere conformity to the Mosaic law or even the Ten Commandments. This is like Saint Augustine's famous dictum, "Love and do what you will." The one living out love concretely need not worry about violating the law, because love orients one's entire life in the direction of the kingdom of God.

The dual images of "running the race" and the yeast that leavens an entire loaf also evoke pastoral and spiritual applications. Just as athletes must train hard to be successful, so must we who accept the gospel message be disciplined in our approach to authentic spirituality. Discipline and sacrifice are essential for successful athletes. This is no less true of believers and those who would seek to grow in the spiritual life (the life of the Spirit). Developing healthy routines of prayer, reflection, and meditation help us maintain the commitment and balance needed to live the gospel message. Followers of Christ do not merely bask in the sunshine of salvation and let the world blithely go on its way. We attempt to grow constantly in the faith we have received at baptism, always seeking to improve the quality of our life, just the way a dedicated athlete strives to achieve new goals.

A third observation concerns the image of the cross. It looms large as ever in the background of the letter. Paul admits that the cross is a stumbling block (*skandalon*, see also 1 Cor 1:23). This has been true since the beginning of Christianity. The early Christians would hardly have made up something as absurd as Jesus's crucifixion were it not an undeniable historical event. Paul is adamant that the cross is front and center in the gospel message. Scandalous and absurd as it may seem, those who live in faith accept the power of the cross. It confirms the hardcore challenge that the Christian life demands—conformity to the cross of Christ, or to use a term some scholars use, "cruciformity" (Gorman). Such a challenging message flies in the face of those who want to proclaim only the message of benefit or success in the Christian life. There are such preachers of the gospel of "profit." Being "blessed" in this world is not necessarily a sign that one's life reflects the true demands of the gospel. The "gospel of success" or "reward" is a seductive Siren who calls the unwary believer down a false path that leads to doom. Lurking behind Paul's instruction for the Galatians is an ardent reminder that people of faith must live in the shadow of the cross.

Fourth, the great contrast between life in the "flesh" and life in the "Spirit" could not be any starker in this section of the letter (5:16–26). If one were to ask, "How do you know if so-and-so is a true Christian?," Paul would answer, "Look at the fruit!" One's actions always betray one's real identity. Actions *always* speak louder than words. Parents know this well when instructing their children. It is difficult to tell children how to live if the parents' actions themselves reveal an alternative. Flesh in this context, of course, represents all that is fleeting and finite in this world. It is a cipher for all that is corruptible. It is the opposite of the Spirit. The life of the Spirit, which characterizes life in the "new creation," is as concrete as the evils that characterize fleshly existence. Both are perceived in concrete attitudes and actions.

Finally, note how Paul connects the proper ethical life not only with personal and individual behavior but also with comportment in the community (6:1–10). True, Christ died for me (as Paul says in 2:20), but he also gave himself up for *us*. Life in the new creation can be none other than that which is lived in harmony in the community of faith. The commandment to love one another and to bear one another's burdens is essential (5:14; 6:2). We might recall, here, Paul's advice to the Corinthian community when he gave them the powerful image of the Body of Christ (1 Cor 12:12–26). He reminds them of the interconnectedness of all the parts of the body so that it may function well. And he says, "If one member suffers, all suffer together with it; if one member is honored, all rejoice together with it" (1 Cor 12:26 NRSV). Bearing and forbearing with and for one another is essential. Paul even sees his ethical instruction as providing an examination of conscience (6:4). We are called to "do good to all" but especially to the "family of faith" (6:10), which is a reminder that Paul never surrendered to the temptation to view the Galatians as *outside* this family of faith. Sad and perplexed though he is at their stubborn attitude, he still views them as members of this family. This should make us consider our own attitudes to those who perhaps do not conform to the ideal of faith. Do we still see them as family, albeit members who have gone, or are in danger of going, astray? Or are we in a hurry to label them outsiders, heretics, evildoers, those excommunicated with whom we want no contact? It is far easier to erect barriers in the community of faith by proscribing those whom we think outside the bounds than it is to reach out and try to invite those on the margins to consider coming closer to the center of the community. Hopefully, in my interpretation of Galatians, it has been clear that Paul never went so far as to consider the Galatians were now outside! He just kept trying to bring them back to their senses.

REFLECTION QUESTIONS

1. How do you understand the concepts of freedom and slavery today? In what ways does your life reflect freedom? Are there any vestiges of being "enslaved" in your life?

2. Paul uses the expression "faith working through love" (5:6). How does this expression jive with the idea of "justification by faith"? What is the relationship between faith and love?

3. What do you make of Paul's sarcastic wish that the agitators would "castrate themselves" (5:12)? How can we reconcile such a sentiment with Jesus's demand to love our enemies (see Matt 5:44)? Does Paul overstep his bounds here? Why or why not?

4. How do you understand Paul's contrast between "flesh" and "Spirit"? Are his accompanying lists of vices to avoid and virtues to foster reasonable? In other words, are Paul's ethical expectations realistic? Can you create a list of modern vices and virtues?

5. What role does an "examination of conscience" play in your own spiritual life? How do you evaluate your life objectively? What "checks and balances" help you to focus on the values of the Christian life?

6. How do you think Christians should treat other Christians who hold to immoral or unethical teachings? What can be done to convince them of right from wrong? Does holding out hope for wayward Christians promote ethical laxity? Is it possible to "condemn the sin" but "love the sinner"? How might Paul react to such a challenge?

6

THE CLOSING (6:11–18)

Although this closing section bears some similarity to other closing sections of Paul's letters in its use of certain formulae (e.g., 1 Thess 5:28; Phil 4:23; Phlm 25; Rom 15:33), it is not merely a formality.[1] Like the greeting, the closing is intimately tied to the context of this specific letter. Paul brings his forceful letter to a conclusion in two quick stages:

A Final Plea (6:11–17)

A Final Greeting (6:18)

THE CLOSING (6:11–18)

[11] See what large letters I make when I am writing in my own hand! [12] It is those who want to make a good showing in the flesh that try to compel you to be circumcised—only so that they may not be persecuted for the cross of Christ. [13] For not even the circumcised themselves obey the law, but they want you to be circumcised so that they may boast about your flesh. [14] May I never boast of anything except the cross of our Lord Jesus Christ, through which the world has been crucified to me, and I to the world. [15] For neither circumcision nor uncircumcision is anything; but new creation! [16] As for those who will follow this rule—peace be upon them and mercy, also upon the Israel of God. [17] Finally, let no one cause me trouble; for I carry on my body the marks of Jesus. [18] May the grace of our Lord Jesus Christ be with your spirit, brothers and sisters. Amen.

---

1 Cor 2:2; 7:19; 5:17
Pss 125:5; 128:6
1 Cor 16:21; 2 Cor 4:10; Phil 4:23; 2 Tim 4:22; Phlm 2

The closing (vv. 11–17) contains some expressions that serve as reminders for the main message Paul has attempted to communicate in his letter, as well as more personal information that can help reinforce the message. As Paul began the letter with personal testimony

(1:1, 11–24), so he ends it likewise calling to mind personal information (especially vv. 14 and 17). Paul begins the closing in very personal fashion, writing in his own hand (v. 11; also 1 Cor 16:21). Whether the reference to "large letters" refers to letter size or the lack of good penmanship, Paul's ability apparently lacked the refined style of a scribe (amanuensis) whose services he regularly employed when dictating letters (e.g., Tertius in Rom 16:22). Alternatively, some scholars speculate that Paul had poor eyesight (see the reference to eyes at 4:15) and thus wrote in abnormally large letters, or that he wanted to emphasize something, like using bold print today. Regardless, it personalizes the letter and provides emphasis. Recent research, indeed, has shown that this was not an unusual practice in antiquity. It indicates two facts: (1) most writers employed professional secretaries, as did Paul, and thus were not that adept at writing themselves; and (2) such a "signature" helped to authenticate the letter.[2]

Then he reiterates several aspects of his message as a final plea. First, he draws attention to the desire on the part of the opponents to "boast" in compelling the Galatians to be circumcised. The vocabulary of "boasting" (*kauchaomai*; see 2 Cor 10:12–18) is one of Paul's favorite expressions.[3] Normally, it is pejorative. It refers to self-boasting or recommending oneself. But Paul understands another kind of boasting, that which comes externally; it is boasting "in the Lord" (1 Cor 1:31; 2 Cor 10:17). In Galatians, Paul accuses the agitators of wanting to boast in the Galatians' flesh, using the expression literally (soft tissue), and metaphorically (a cipher for circumcision). Paul even claims their motivation may have been to avoid persecution by being circumcised, since the Romans granted special status to Jews due to their religious beliefs. This would essentially help them avoid being "persecuted for the cross of Christ," something in which Paul glories (lit. "boasts," i.e., the proper way of doing it; 2 Cor 12:17). Paul insists, "May I never boast of anything except the cross of our Lord Jesus Christ, through which the world has been crucified to me, and I to the world."

The Stigmata

From at least the Middle Ages, there have been holy women and men who are believed to have received a remarkable and mysterious spiritual "gift" of the stigmata (from Greek *stigma*, "mark" or "brand"), the physical signs corresponding to the wounds Christ received on his hands, feet, and side from his crucifixion. These five bodily wounds, from which blood usually seeps and which, in each case, do not always appear in the same location of the body, were traditionally taken as an indication of holiness and closeness to Christ.

The most famous figure to receive the stigmata is Saint Francis of Assisi (ca. 1181-1226), who experienced the phenomenon during a mystical experience in 1224 near the end of his life. Saint Catherine of Siena (1347-80), the mystic and doctor of the Church, was said to have had an "invisible" stigmata. There have been hundreds of other cases of the stigmata claimed since in Church history, most among women. In modern times, Saint Padre Pio of Pietrelcina (1887–1968) is one who was said to have had the phenomenon. Whatever its origin, the experience of the stigmata defies scientific explanation, but the Catholic Church refrains from making formal pronouncements about the authenticity of specific cases. Spiritually, these marks are signs of the suffering that often accompanies the gospel of Jesus Christ.

St. Francis of Assisi Receiving the Stigmata by Peter Paul Rubens (ca. 1630 CE)

Paul's identification with Christ on the cross, as he had earlier shown (2:20), is complete. Metaphorically, he has been "crucified" with Christ. Indeed, he speaks of the marks (*stigmata*) he bears on his body (v. 17), reminiscent of the brand marks placed on the bodies of slaves to identify their owner. Here, it does not refer to "stigmata" as it came to be known in later Christian tradition—the marks of crucifixion in the hands, feet, and side of Jesus—but the sufferings, physical and otherwise, Paul has had to bear in the course of his ministry for the sake of the gospel (2 Cor 11:22–28; also 2 Cor 4:10), including his present prickly relationship with the wayward Galatians. The beauty of this expression is that it offers an alternative to the Galatians who have been tempted to revert to another "mark" of identity: circumcision. Paul, rather, is marked by the cross (2:19–20). He then repeats the view he had stated earlier that neither circumcision nor uncircumcision counts for anything; only "new creation" counts (*kainē ktisis*; cf. 2 Cor 5:17). Paul affirms the utter newness that has come to those who live "in Christ." We are nothing short of "new creation," God accomplishing something totally new in humanity through the power of the cross and resurrection of Jesus Christ. The expectation of a new universe was, in fact, a vision already proclaimed in the OT and now, in the Christian dispensation, fulfilled in Christ (Isa 65:17–25). If Paul does not use the vocabulary of new creation frequently, there is no doubt that it looms large in his overall theological vision. What has happened in Christ is totally new, and all who are born in him through baptism and the Spirit are also new: they have a chance to begin again.

New Creation

The notion that God would ultimately form a new creation has OT roots. It is rooted in Jewish apocalyptic expectation that God would act favorably at the "end time" to form a new creation. Already in the time of Third Isaiah (Isa 65:17–25), the postexilic prophet of hope and restoration, such an image emerges, as seen in the following two quotations:

> For I am about to create new heavens
>   and a new earth;
> the former things shall not be remembered
>   or come to mind. (Isa 65:17 NRSV)

> For as the new heavens and the new earth,
>   which I will make,
> shall remain before me, says the LORD;
>   so shall your descendants and your name remain.

> (Isa 66:22 NRSV; some OT Apocrypha also mention the
> concept, such as Jubilees, 1 Enoch, 4 Ezra, and 2 Baruch)

This hopeful image is reflected in the Book of Revelation, which also speaks of a "new heaven and a new earth" (21:1) and in Second Peter (3:13). Obviously, this language has an apocalyptic sense, speaking of the end times, after God's judgment has passed and true justice will be established in all creation.

The term "new creation" (see also 2 Cor 5:17) is a special Pauline expression to speak of the entire transformation that comes about when one enters, by baptism, the new life of Christ. Previous barriers to human interaction fall away (Gal 3:28); we become reconciled to God and to one another (2 Cor 5:17-20); the new replaces the old, and humanity has the chance again to return to the pristine condition God had always intended by his original act of creation (Gen 1–2). The concept also relates to Paul's larger apocalyptic outlook. The new creation will ultimately take the place of the "present evil age" (Gal 1:4) when the life of the Spirit will come to full fruition and all the effects of the salvation achieved by Jesus Christ will be accomplished in full.

Here in Galatians, the expression is intended to draw the Galatians back to their senses, recognizing the gift that God has already given them and the freedom that has come with it and that already constitutes an inauguration into the new creation. Because they participate in the new creation, they need no other supports for their life, no other identity markers, no other obligations. All they need do is live according to the Spirit. (Cf. Owens).

There is another aspect to verse 15 that is especially evident in the Greek text. Here, Paul notes the same pairing of circumcision and uncircumcision that he had mentioned in a different context in 5:6. The parallels are more evident with this more literal translation and the Greek words transliterated:

> For [*gar*] in Christ Jesus there is neither circumcision [*oute peritomē ti*] nor uncircumcision [*oute akrobystia*] but [*alla*] faith working through love. (5:6)
>
> For [*gar*] neither circumcision [*oute peritomē ti*] nor uncircumcision [*oute akrobystia*] has power but [*alla*] new creation! (6:15)

In the first sentence, where the key phrase is "in Christ Jesus," Paul sets out to explain freedom and the importance of (our) faith. This is where we find our new identity through baptism, and we show it forth by our "faith working through love." In Christ, circumcision or uncircumcision count for nothing. What counts (the strong adversative conjunction "but" [*alla*]) is putting our faith in loving action.[4] In the second instance, as Paul is about to conclude the letter, he evokes formally the image of "new creation," but calls to mind once more for the Galatians the contrast between circumcision and uncircumcision. What it means to be in Christ Jesus is nothing less than becoming a new creation (again, the strong adversative "but"). By drawing these parallels, Paul reinforces his gospel message that, in Christ, everything has changed.

Paul also wishes "peace" and "mercy" (*eleos*)[5] to the Galatians, but we must carefully note the construction of this greeting. He begins with "As for those who will follow this rule—peace be upon them." Then he adds, "and mercy, also upon the Israel of God." Are the rule followers and the Israel of God separate or the same? Nowhere else does Paul speak of "mercy" at the *end* of a letter. Perhaps his appeal, here, is hope that his letter has sufficiently brought the Galatians to their senses that they will indeed receive inner peace for coming to their senses. He also invokes God's mercy upon "the Israel of God" (v. 16). This expression is not found elsewhere in Paul or in the Hebrew Bible. Scholars debate its meaning. Is "Israel" the people of the covenant, the Jewish people? Not likely. It would be strange for Paul to revert to such an expression after he has insisted that belonging to Christ breaks down such identities (3:28). Moreover, Paul can distinguish between historical Israel and spiritual Israel (implied in 1 Cor 10:18 and perhaps Rom 9:6b). Is it the new people of God, the Christian family? Considering that Paul has been combatting a Jewish-oriented opposition to the gospel message, this is more likely, although the expression of the Church as the "new Israel" does not appear in Christianity until the mid-second century CE. Paul's point seems to be that those who walk in the ways of the Spirit—who will follow this rule—are now the Israel of God. Paul wishes God's peace and mercy upon them. In a sense, he reaffirms that they become a "new creation" by their willingness to live out their new identity in which circumcision and uncircumcision, as well as other distinctions, no longer hold any value.

The final line (v. 18) closes the letter without any specific greetings—unlike some of Paul's other letters (Rom 16:3–16; 1 Thess 5:26; Col 4:15–17)—but with a typically Pauline benediction or blessing, wishing "the grace of our Lord Jesus Christ" upon the Galatians. Essentially, what Paul has been debating all along is God's grace at work in the Galatians, even when they were wayward children who knew not their real identity. As one commentator puts it, "Paul has argued and rebuked and cajoled, but his last word is GRACE, for him the only word that really mattered" (Barclay, 57, emphasis original). In addition, despite the sharp tones Paul has sometimes used throughout the letter to challenge his opponents and those Galatians who are being seduced by them, the next to last word, just before "Amen,"[6] is "brothers and sisters" (*adelphoi*), a rare expression for Paul at the conclusion of his letters.[7] To the end, Paul holds out the promise that the Galatians will ultimately prove to be faithful members of God's household. They will return to the fold. We do not know how effective Paul's letter was among them. The very preservation of the letter in the Pauline corpus, however, would indicate that many in the Pauline communities valued its teaching and thus preserved it for all future Christian generations. Its powerful message of freedom in Christ Jesus lives on. Life in the new creation cannot be easily defeated with God's grace at work among those who receive the message.

PASTORAL AND SPIRITUAL OBSERVATIONS

Paul ends his letter with another personal appeal, taking the time, or making the effort, to sign it in his own hand. Perhaps he hoped that this last gesture would again get the Galatians' attention. In this letter, Paul never ceases being a concerned "parent" for his wayward children in the faith. He also reminds them—and us—that staying faithful in Christ is not an easy task. He recalls the cross—that essential Christian symbol that always brings us back to the reason for, and means of, our salvation. If we want to boast of anything, it should be that we are proud of the cross and what is represents. Perhaps we wear it as jewelry around our necks, or we display it publicly in our homes, our churches, and our schools. But it should never become a mere decoration or an empty symbol. Wherever it is displayed, it is a reminder of the love of God that knows no bounds. It is the only symbol in which we should glory; it is the sign of faithfulness of Christ, who suffered and died so that the world might have new life and become a new creation.

Complete Attachment to Christ

John Calvin captures clearly the importance of newness, becoming totally a new creation, in Paul's thought (Gal 6:15), by the complete attachment to Christ. He explains,

> The reason why he [Paul] is crucified to the world, and the world to him, is that in Christ, to whom he is spiritually united, nothing but a new creature is of any avail. Everything else must be dismissed, must perish. I refer to those things which hinder the renewing of the Spirit. "If anyone be in Christ," says he, "let him be a new creature" (2 Cor 5:17). That is, if any one wishes to be considered as belonging to the kingdom of Christ, let him be created anew by the Spirit of God; let him not live any longer to himself or to the world, but let him be raised up to "newness of life" (Rom 6:4). (Calvin, 168)

Verse 15 is virtually an understatement that brings Paul's argument to a conclusion. It is the punchline that unifies the letter and provides the most far-reaching application of Paul's message. Neither circumcision nor uncircumcision count for anything in terms of our Christian identity, "but new creation." Life in the new creation is a changed life. It is not business as usual. Those who accept this newness live having been marked by the sign of the cross, trusting that it will also lead to the new life found in the resurrection. Paul draws attention to this "branding" with the reference to the marks on his body, both literally and figuratively. Likely, he refers to his sufferings as an apostle (2 Cor 11:23b–28), and in the contemporary world it is worth recalling the innumerable sufferings of Christians throughout the world who have been persecuted, beaten, and even martyred because of their faith. We should probably emphasize here that Paul is not calling on the Galatians to seek physical suffering actively for the sake of the cross of Christ. It is not a matter of pride to want to be persecuted. Rather he simply acknowledges that the cross of Christ in which he boasts has often brought revulsion, rejection, and persecution. When such abuse comes, it must be recognized as an occasion to join our sufferings to those of Christ. This has already begun in baptism, when we accepted to "die" with Christ in order to live with him (2:19; Rom 6:6).

Finally, Paul prayerfully wishes his readers and hearers peace and grace, two of the characteristics with which he opens and closes his letters. But there is a novel element here: mercy. Why mercy? Perhaps because he fears that his instruction will ultimately fall on deaf ears. Maybe his argumentation will have been in vain, as the runner who does not make it to the victory lap (5:7; Phil 2:16). If that is the case, then the Galatians will indeed need God's mercy because they will not have accepted the "new creation" graciously offered to them.

REFLECTION QUESTIONS

1. Does Paul end his letter to the Galatians on a positive note? Do you think he believes the Galatians will heed his message? Why or why not?
2. Summarize "life in the new creation." What are the essential and nonessential characteristics of this life?
3. How does one "boast in the Lord" without appearing to be self-righteous?
4. In what way do you bear witness to the cross of Christ? Have you ever been ridiculed for this witness and, if so, what was your reaction?
5. What "marks" of the Christian life do you bear? Are there ways in which others can easily identify you as a follower of Christ?

AFTERWORD

It is unusual to end a commentary with an afterword. The reason, however, is easily explained. Given that this book is a "spiritual-pastoral" commentary, throughout the various sections of the letter, I have offered spiritual and pastoral reflections based on my interpretation of the text. This has also influenced my choice of quotations from other commentaries, as well as the illustrations and sidebars.

At this point, if you have not already done so, read the Letter to the Galatians in its entirety to appreciate more fully Paul's message (see appendix I) and the spiritual and pastoral "learnings" that emerge from this powerful letter. What follows is my overview of these spiritual and pastoral perspectives.

SPIRITUAL PERSPECTIVES

There are multiple spiritual messages to be gleaned from Galatians. These messages may include the following:

Although the letter contains emotion and polemic, Paul begins and ends—as he does in all his letters—with prayerful references (1:1–5; 6:18). Christian conversations, even difficult ones, should be conducted within a prayerful context rather than through debates or arguments.

Paul never loses sight of the presence of God in the conversation. God is both the source of his ministry (1:1, 11–12) and the source of the Galatians' call (1:6). This "theological" focus aligns with Paul's Jewish monotheism—belief in the one and only God of Israel (3:20). The fact that there is also a trinitarian dimension (including Jesus Christ and the Spirit) in no way detracts from this monotheistic outlook. For Paul, the Trinity is part of the Christian tradition, the way Christians have, since the beginning, understood God's revelation as Father (1:1), Son (2:20), and Holy Spirit (3:3–5).

Paul expresses an openness to, and appreciation of, what we can only describe as "mystical" experiences. When he speaks of revelation (1:12; 2:2) or God "revealing" his Son to him (1:16), or when he speaks metaphorically of being "crucified with Christ" (2:19), or the "world being crucified to me, and I to the world" (6:14), we enter the realm of profound religious experience that is difficult to express. It is Paul's attempt, however, to show the Galatians that their temptation to revert to the "elemental spirits of the world" (4:3) or to accept circumcision is, in fact, a flight from authentic spiritual experience according to God's grace. Life in the Spirit demands that they avoid reverting to slavery.

The Letter to the Galatians also shows Paul's appreciation for the word of God (the multiple OT citations used, some with extensive application, especially from the Abraham story) and the sacramental life of the faith community (6:10, "the household of faith"). His multiple citations show great familiarity with the OT, the word of God, and his emphasis on baptism resonates with basic Christian teaching. Thus, Paul is devoted to Word and Sacrament, two of the essential characteristics of Christian identity, which Vatican Council II reemphasized in its teachings. Furthermore, Galatians is replete with explicit and implicit imagery concerning baptism. If Paul does not explain this sacrament of initiation as fully as he does elsewhere (cf. Rom 6:3–4; 1 Cor 1:13–17; 12:13), he nonetheless connects this sacrament with the changed identity of the Galatians, who, by grace, have entered into Christ Jesus. They have entered the "new creation" (see also the reference to "newness of life" in Rom 6:4, and the unity of all who are in Christ in 1 Cor 12:13). Word and Sacrament together shape our lives no less today than in Paul's day.

Clearly, the spiritual message Paul insists on in his letter to the Galatians is the cross of Christ (5:11; 6:14) and the effects it has wrought. His entire argument is based upon the power of the cross, with "crucifixion" being both a literal reference to what happened to Jesus of Nazareth and a spiritual call to renounce the attractions of this world ("flesh") and to follow the life of the Spirit that flows from the cross. In other words, Paul summons the Galatians to a profound reflection at the foot of the cross.

Another spiritual theme at the core of the letter is the contrast between justification by faith and our good works. Here, admittedly, some differences are bound to persist in dialogues between Protestants and Catholics. As a Roman Catholic, I do not believe that justification is *the* centerpiece of Paul's theology.[1] It is one among several distinct but interrelated themes tied to the effects that have come from the "Christ event," especially the incarnation, the cross, and the resurrection. Thus, justification—whether being declared or made right by God's grace—is fully the action of God, God's gracious outreach to sinful humanity. Accompanying it are also redemption, salvation, reconciliation, and sanctification. Christ's fidelity to his Father's will has accomplished this, and he invites us into this accomplishment by making us heirs as well. God's action of salvation was once and for all (cf. Rom 6:10; see also Heb 7:27; 10:10; 1 Pet 3:18), but the effects continue even as we await the fullness of sanctification in the kingdom. Important for Roman Catholics to note, however, is that the good works we are called to do are not *to obtain* salvation but are outward signs of having accepted God's gift of salvation that is freely given.

One cannot leave out another aspect of Paul's spirituality, namely the call to live the life of the Spirit, whose primary fruit is love, which leads to a multitude of virtues (5:22). Our faith *in* Christ leads to following the "law of Christ" (6:2), which demands living the upright life for which we will one day be held accountable (6:7–9; cf. 5:21). Consequently, there is an ethical dimension to Paul's spirituality, influenced also by his apocalyptic outlook. Spirituality is not simply prayer and worship; it involves "love in action," or rather "faith working through love" (5:6). Indeed, in this context, Paul's clarion call to live the life of the Spirit as free individuals is a reminder that God's grace never *forces* us to act in accord with the higher law of love. Nor does it limit us to following individual commands of the law. Paul insists that the Spirit has bestowed full freedom upon the Galatians; they would be fools to throw it all away!

PASTORAL PERSPECTIVES

If these are some of the key insights from Paul's spiritual teaching in his letter to the Galatians, what pastoral principles can we discern in the letter?

First, notice that Paul, without ever using the term, acts as a true "pastor" to the Galatians. He is even more than their shepherd, however, concerned that they not be led astray or wander away from the "truth of the gospel." He also presents himself as their parent, employing especially the tender image of a mother trying to give birth to worthy sons and daughters but wondering how they will turn out. They remain his children despite their wayward ways (4:19).

As any good pastor knows, Paul also walks the tightrope of both affirming his charges and challenging them. If one only preached the "good news" one wants to hear, the flock would be appeased. But the cross of Christ would be robbed of its true value (6:14). He affirms their one-time kindness toward him (4:14), but also goes so far as to call them "foolish" or "stupid" (3:1) because of what he has heard they are doing in abandoning the one and only gospel of Christ. On the one hand, he affirms them consistently throughout the letter as "brothers and sisters" and calls them, by virtue of their new baptismal identity, to break down any divisions that remain in their midst (3:28). Yet, on the other hand, he expresses perplexity as to whether they will heed his word (4:20). This is a true pastor at work. At one and the same time, he tries to affirm and cajole, praise and exhort, appease and push. Like any pastor of a congregation who must move on to other ministry, Paul cannot be certain, at a distance, that the seeds he has planted in Galatia will bear the kind of fruit they should (cf. 1 Cor 3:6).

Another noteworthy pastoral practice is Paul's use of certain conventions of his day to strengthen his argumentation. Thus, he references sports imagery, uses Jewish and Greco-Roman rhetorical devices, and draws attention to common realities of the day (wills, slavery, pedagogues, etc.). Pastorally, Paul seems willing to use whatever is available in the standard culture that will make his point more effective. A good preacher knows well the importance of not just expounding the word. He or she must also find ways to make it understandable. The Christian faith is not always opposed to every aspect of culture but sometimes makes good use of it. Even the letter format provided Paul a way to stay in touch with the communities he founded or became acquainted with. One wonders what use he would have made of the Internet and social media!

A more challenging aspect is the relationship between Paul's theology and his pastoral practice. One must read between the lines to discern this dimension, but it is present in the Letter to the Galatians. In brief, Paul wrote the letter out of pastoral necessity, to address from a distance a problem that had arisen in his beloved Galatian communities. The letter is a clarion call to return to the freedom of the gospel by rejecting the allure of the agitators to accept circumcision. Paul does this with strong language, exhortation, and some fancy rhetorical argumentation. Amid this pastoral enterprise, however, one can see Paul bringing his theological perspective to bear on the situation. It is not merely an "ivory tower" theology. It is based upon personal experience (1:12; 2:19–20). If Galatians is indeed one of Paul's earlier letters, then one sees him struggling here to express what "the faith of Jesus Christ" really means for him and for his communities. Christ's own fidelity, especially in accepting the cross, has shown us the path. That same path leads us to a life of faith *in* Christ, with all its attendant demands to live the law of love. Paul was fleshing this out in heated conversation with the Galatians. In doing so, he was bringing his own theological insight to bear on the pastoral problem he faced. Two thousand years later, we are the beneficiaries of this encounter that shows us that theology is indeed important for the pastoral life, but that it also can be shaped amid that same context.

CONCLUSION

Hopefully, these spiritual and pastoral perspectives from Galatians will spur your own reflections. By exploring this brief but intense letter from the Pauline corpus, one enters the world of the first great Christian pastoral theologian, Paul the Apostle.

An American Episcopal priest, Robert Farrar Capon (1925–2013), who was a prolific and creative author, once quipped, "The Gospels were written for the sake of the Pauline Epistles."[2] Ironically, the Gospels were written well after Paul's letters, but the quip contains a truth: Paul's deep reflections on the meaning of the gospel message gave impetus and depth to the spread of that "good news" of hope and salvation. His letters open the door, but they also lead to the same end: an encounter with the risen Lord Christ Jesus, the very same one he had encountered on the road to Damascus. We owe a great debt to "the Apostle" that is hopefully evident in this commentary.

PAUL'S LETTER TO THE GALATIANS

A Translation

1 ¹ Paul an apostle—not from human beings nor by human authority, but through Jesus Christ and God the Father, who raised him from the dead— ² and all the brothers and sisters who are with me, to the churches of Galatia: ³ Grace to you and peace from God the Father and our Lord Jesus Christ, ⁴ who gave himself for our sins in order to rescue us from the present evil age, according to the will of our God and Father, ⁵ to whom be glory forever and ever. Amen.

⁶ I am astonished that you are turning away so quickly from the one who called you in the grace of Christ for a different gospel— ⁷ not that there is another one—but there are some people who are disturbing you and wanting to pervert the gospel of Christ. ⁸ But even if we or an angel from heaven should proclaim to you a gospel contrary to the one we proclaimed to you, let that person be accursed! ⁹ As we said before, and now I say again, if anyone proclaims to you a gospel contrary to what you have received, let that person be accursed! ¹⁰ For, am I now appealing to human beings, or to God? Or am I trying to please human beings? If I were still trying to please human beings, I would not be a slave of Christ.

¹¹ For I want you to know, brothers and sisters, that the gospel proclaimed by me is not of human origin; ¹² neither did I receive it from a human source, nor was I taught it, but I received it through a revelation of Jesus Christ.

¹³ For you have heard, no doubt, of my former life in Judaism, that I was persecuting the church of God to an extraordinary degree and, in fact, was trying to destroy it. ¹⁴ And I advanced in Judaism far beyond many of the contemporaries of my race, for I was a far more zealous adherent of the traditions handed down from my ancestors. ¹⁵ But when the One who had set me apart from my mother's womb and called me by his grace was pleased ¹⁶ to reveal his Son to me, in order that I might proclaim him to the gentiles, I did not immediately consult any human being, ¹⁷ nor did I go up to Jerusalem to those who were already apostles before me; rather I went away into Arabia, and [then] returned again to Damascus.

¹⁸ Then after three years I went up to Jerusalem to get acquainted with Cephas and stayed with him fifteen days; ¹⁹ but I did not see any other apostle except James, the brother of the Lord. ²⁰ (In what I am writing to you, I assure you before God, I am not lying!) ²¹ Then I came to the regions of Syria and Cilicia, ²² but I was still unknown by sight to the churches of Judea that are in Christ; ²³ they only were hearing it said, "The one who formerly was persecuting us is now proclaiming the faith he had earlier tried to destroy." ²⁴ And they glorified God because of me.

---

2 ¹ Then after fourteen years I went up again to Jerusalem with Barnabas, taking Titus along also. ² I went up because of a revelation, and I laid out to them (though only in a private meeting with the acknowledged leaders) the gospel that I preach among the gentiles, lest somehow, I was running, or had run, in vain. ³ But not even Titus, who was with me, although he was a Greek, was compelled to be circumcised. ⁴ Now because of certain false brothers secretly brought in, who slipped in to spy on our freedom that we have in Christ Jesus, so that they might enslave us— ⁵ we did not submit to them even for a moment, so that the truth of the gospel might always remain intact with you. ⁶ But from those who were reputed leaders (what they actually were makes no difference to me; God shows no partiality)—for those leaders contributed nothing to me. ⁷ On the contrary, when they saw that I had been entrusted with the gospel for the uncircumcised, just as Peter had been entrusted the same for the circumcised ⁸ (for the one who was at work through Peter, making him an apostle to the circumcised, also worked through me for the gentiles), ⁹ and when James and Cephas and John, who were reputed pillars, recognized the grace that had been given to me, they gave to me and Barnabas the right hand of fellowship, in order that we should go to the gentiles and they to the circumcision. ¹⁰ They asked only one thing, namely, that we remember the poor, the very thing I was also eager to do.

¹¹ But when Cephas came to Antioch, I opposed him to his face, because he stood self-condemned; ¹² for until certain people came from James, he used to eat with the gentiles. But after they came, he withdrew and kept himself separate for fear of the circumcision faction, ¹³ and the rest of the Jews also joined him in this hypocrisy, so that even Barnabas was carried away with them in their hypocrisy. ¹⁴ But when I saw that they were not being straightforward with the truth of the gospel, I said to Cephas before them all, "If you, though a Jew, live like a gentile and not like a Jew, how can you compel the gentiles to live like Jews?"

¹⁵ We ourselves are Jews by birth and not "gentile sinners"; ¹⁶ yet knowing that a person is justified not by the works of the law but by faith in Jesus Christ. And we have believed in Christ Jesus, so that we may be justified by the faith of Christ, and not by the works of the law, because no human being will be justified by the works of the law. ¹⁷ If, however, in our effort to be justified in Christ, we ourselves also have been found to be sinners, is Christ then a servant of sin? By no means! ¹⁸ For if I build up again the very things that I once tore down, then I show myself to be a transgressor. ¹⁹ For through the law I died

to the law, so that I might live to God. I have been crucified with Christ; [20] yet I no longer live, but Christ lives in me. And the life I now live in the flesh I live by faith in the Son of God, who loved me and gave himself for me. [21] I do not nullify the grace of God; for if justification comes through the law, then Christ died for nothing.

---

3 [1] O foolish Galatians! Who has bewitched you, before whose eyes Jesus Christ was publicly exhibited as crucified? [2] The only thing I want to learn from you is this: Did you receive the Spirit by doing the works of the law or by believing what you heard? [3] Are you so foolish? Having begun by the Spirit, are you now ending with the flesh? [4] Did you experience so much in vain?—if it really was in vain! [5] Therefore, does the one who gives you the Spirit and works miracles among you do so by the works of the law, or by your believing what you heard?

[6] Just as Abraham "believed God, and it was reckoned to him as righteousness," [7] so, understand, those who have faith are the descendants of Abraham. [8] And the scripture, foreseeing that God would justify the gentiles by faith, proclaimed the gospel beforehand to Abraham, saying, "All the gentiles shall be blessed in you." [9] So then, those who have faith are blessed together with Abraham who believed. [10] For all who rely on the works of the law are under a curse; for it is written, "Cursed is everyone who does not observe and do all the things written in the book of the law." [11] Now it is clear that no one is justified before God by the law; for "the one who is righteous will live by faith." [12] But the law does not come from faith; on the contrary, "Whoever does these things will live by them." [13] Christ redeemed us from the curse of the law by becoming a curse for us—for it is written, "Cursed is everyone who hangs on a tree"— [14] in order that in Christ Jesus the blessing of Abraham might come to the gentiles, so that we might receive the promise of the Spirit through faith.

[15] Brothers and sisters, let me speak from a human perspective: once a person's will has been ratified, no one adds to it or annuls it. [16] Now the promises were made to Abraham and to his descendant; it does not say, "and to [his] descendants," as concerning many; but it says, "and to your offspring," that is, to one person, who is Christ. [17] My point is this: the law, which came 430 years later, does not revoke a covenant previously ratified by God, so as to nullify the promise. [18] For if the inheritance comes from the law, it no longer comes from the promise; but God graciously gave it to Abraham through the promise. [19] Why then the law? It was added because of transgressions, until the descendant would come to whom the promise had been made; and it was ordained through angels by the hand of a mediator. [20] Now a mediator involves more than one party; but God is one. [21] Therefore is the law opposed to the promises of God? By no means! For if a law had been given that was able to give life, then righteousness would indeed come through the law. [22] But the scripture imprisoned all under the power of sin, so that what was promised by faith in Jesus Christ might be given to those who believe.

[23] Now before faith came, we were detained under the law, and imprisoned until the coming faith would be revealed. [24] Therefore the law was our disciplinarian until Christ

came, so that we might be justified by faith. ²⁵ But now that faith has come, we are no longer under a disciplinarian, ²⁶ for you are all children of God through faith in Christ Jesus. ²⁷ As many of you as were baptized into Christ have clothed yourselves with Christ. ²⁸ There is no longer Jew or Greek, there is no longer slave or free, there is no longer male and female; for all of you are one in Christ Jesus. ²⁹ And if you are Christ's, then you are Abraham's descendants, heirs according to a promise.

---

4 ¹ So this is my point: as long as the heir is a child, he is no better than a slave, even though he is the master of everything; ² rather, he remains under guardians and managers until the date set by the father. ³ So it is with us; when we were children, we were enslaved by the elemental spirits of the world. ⁴ But when the fullness of time had come, God sent his Son, born of a woman, born under the law, ⁵ in order that he might redeem those under the law, so that we might receive adoption. ⁶ And because you are children, God has sent the Spirit of his Son into our hearts, crying, "*Abba*! Father!" ⁷ So you are no longer a slave but a child, and if a child then also an heir, through God. ⁸ But formerly, when you did not know God, you were enslaved to beings that by nature are not gods. ⁹ However, now that you have come to know God—or rather to be known by God—how can you turn back again to the weak and impotent elemental spirits? Do you want to be enslaved to them all over again? ¹⁰ You observe special days, and months, and seasons, and years. ¹¹ I am afraid that I may have labored for you in vain!

¹² Brothers and sisters, I beg you, become as I am, for I also have become as you are. You have done me no wrong. ¹³ Now you know that it was due to an illness of mine that I first preached the gospel to you; ¹⁴ though my condition was a trial for you, you did not scorn or despise me, but welcomed me as an angel of God, like Christ Jesus. ¹⁵ So where is your blessing now? For I testify that, had it been possible, you would have torn out your eyes and given them to me. ¹⁶ So have I now become your enemy by telling you the truth? ¹⁷ They zealously court you, but not commendably; for they want to exclude you, so that you may zealously court them. ¹⁸ It is good to be courted zealously to good purpose at all times, and not only when I am present with you. ¹⁹ My children, for whom I am again in the pain of childbirth until Christ is formed in you! ²⁰ I wish I were present with you now and could change my tone, for I am perplexed about you.

²¹ Tell me, you who desire to be under the law, do you not understand the law? ²² For it is written that Abraham had two sons, one by a slave woman and the other by a free woman. ²³ One, the child of the slave, was born according to the flesh; the other, the child of the free woman, was born through a promise. ²⁴ Now this is an allegory, for these women are two covenants. One, who is Hagar, is from Mount Sinai, bearing children for slavery. ²⁵ Now Hagar is Mount Sinai in Arabia and corresponds to the present Jerusalem, for she is a slave with her children. ²⁶ But the other woman corresponds to the Jerusalem above; she is free, and she is our mother. ²⁷ For it is written, "Rejoice, you barren woman, who does not give birth, / burst into song and shout, you who endure no birth pangs, / for the children of

the desolate woman / are more numerous than the children of the one who has a husband." [28] Now you, my brothers and sisters, are children of a promise, just like Isaac. [29] But just as at that time the child who was born according to the flesh persecuted the child who was born according to the Spirit, so it is now also. [30] But what does the scripture say? "Drive out the slave woman and her child; for the child of the slave woman will not share the inheritance with the child of the free woman." [31] So then, brothers and sisters, we are children, not of the slave but of the free woman.

---

5 [1] For freedom, Christ has set us free. Stand firm, therefore, and do not submit again to a yoke of slavery. [2] Look! I, Paul, am telling you that if you let yourselves be circumcised, Christ will be of no benefit to you. [3] Once again, I testify to every man who lets himself be circumcised that he is obliged to keep the entire law. [4] You who want to be justified by the law have cut yourselves off from Christ; you have fallen away from grace. [5] For through the Spirit, by faith, we eagerly wait for the hope of righteousness. [6] For in Christ Jesus neither circumcision nor uncircumcision counts for anything; the only thing that counts is faith working through love.

[7] You were running well; who hindered you from obeying the truth? [8] Such persuasion does not come from the one who calls you. [9] A little yeast leavens the whole batch of dough. [10] I am confident about you in the Lord that you will not think otherwise. But whoever is confusing you will pay the penalty. [11] Now, brothers and sisters, if I am still preaching circumcision, why am I still being persecuted? In that case the stumbling block of the cross has been removed. [12] I wish those who are disturbing you would also castrate themselves!

[13] For you were called to freedom, brothers and sisters; only do not use your freedom as an opportunity for the flesh, but through love become servants to one another. [14] For the whole law is summed up in one commandment, namely, "You shall love your neighbor as yourself." [15] If, however, you bite and devour one another, watch out that you are not consumed by one another! [16] But I say, live by the Spirit, and do not gratify the desires of the flesh. [17] For what the flesh desires is opposed to the Spirit, and what the Spirit desires is opposed to the flesh; for these are opposed to each other, to prevent you from doing what you want. [18] But if you are led by the Spirit, you are not under the law. [19] Now the works of the flesh are obvious: sexual immorality, impurity, licentiousness, [20] idolatry, sorcery, enmities, strife, jealousy, anger, quarrels, dissensions, factions, [21] envy, drunkenness, carousing, and things like these. I am warning you, as I warned you before: those who do such things will not inherit the kingdom of God. [22] By contrast, the fruit of the Spirit is love, joy, peace, patience, kindness, generosity, faithfulness, [23] humility, and self-control. There is no law against such things. [24] And those who belong to Christ Jesus have crucified the flesh with its passions and desires. [25] If we live by the Spirit, let us also walk in line with the Spirit. [26] Let us not become conceited, provoking one another, envying one another.

6 [1] Brothers and sisters, even if anyone is caught in a transgression, you who are spiritual should restore such a one in a spirit of gentleness, taking care that you yourself are also not tempted. [2] Bear one another's burdens, and so fulfill the law of Christ. [3] For anyone who thinks he is something, even though he is nothing, deceives himself. [4] Let each person examine their own work; then that work, rather than their neighbor's work, will become a cause for boasting. [5] For all must carry their own burden. [6] The one who is taught the word must share all good things with their teacher. [7] Do not be deceived; God is not mocked, for you reap whatever you sow. [8] If you sow to your own flesh, you will reap corruption from the flesh; but if you sow to the Spirit, you will reap eternal life from the Spirit. [9] So let us not grow weary in doing good, for we will reap at harvest time, if we do not give up. [10] So, then, whenever we have an opportunity, let us work for the good of all, and especially for those of the household of faith.

[11] See what large letters I make when I am writing in my own hand! [12] It is those who want to make a good showing in the flesh that try to compel you to be circumcised—only so that they may not be persecuted for the cross of Christ. [13] For not even the circumcised themselves obey the law, but they want you to be circumcised so that they may boast about your flesh. [14] May I never boast of anything except the cross of our Lord Jesus Christ, through which the world has been crucified to me, and I to the world. [15] For neither circumcision nor uncircumcision is anything; but new creation! [16] As for those who will follow this rule—peace be upon them and mercy, also upon the Israel of God. [17] Finally, let no one cause me trouble; for I carry on my body the marks of Jesus.

[18] May the grace of our Lord Jesus Christ be with your spirit, brothers and sisters. Amen.

GALATIANS IN THE *CATECHISM* OF THE CATHOLIC CHURCH

One of the great achievements of the post–Vatican II era has been the publication of a new compendium of the Catholic faith, the *Catechism of the Catholic Church* (2nd ed.; Rome: Editrice Vaticana, 1998). Pope John Paul II ordered its compilation, and it remains an important authoritative summary of the Catholic faith in modern times. The purpose of this appendix is to provide readers of this commentary with a summary of how Galatians is treated in the *Catechism*.

First, it should be noted that scholarly debates ensued at the publication of the *Catechism* concerning its use of Scripture. For some critics, it is too oriented to "proof texting," that is, using explicit biblical citations to *prove* some aspect of the Catholic faith. While there is some truth to this, we should note that all Christians engage in proof texting in one form or another. The more important question is how far one bends the meaning of Scripture from its literal sense. For the most part, the *Catechism* attempts to present the biblical foundations of the Catholic faith and to point out passages where essential teachings (or the seeds of such teachings) are found. Certainly, one finds apologetic elements in the use of some Pauline citations in the *Catechism*, but overall, it demonstrates how Scripture forms the basis of so many Church teachings.

The following observations provide a summary of the use of the Letter to the Galatians in the *Catechism*. Note that only places where the *Catechism* explicitly cites or mentions a passage are included, and not references used merely as supporting passages.

[1:1] §857 cites Paul's assertion of his apostleship to reiterate that the Church herself is apostolic. This is one of the four key identifying factors of the Church, the other three being its oneness, holiness, and catholicity (universality). The early Christian creeds (e.g., Nicene-Constantinople), accepted by many Christian denominations, assert these four marks of the Church universal (see also *CCC* §§811–70).

[1:4] §2824 uses Paul's expression to reinforce the importance of fulfilling God's will, a duty of all Christians.

[1:15–16] The *Catechism* associates this passage of Paul's commission to preach the gospel of Jesus Christ with his acknowledgment of Jesus as Son of God (§442).

[2:20] §478 cites Paul's personal statement of Christ's love for him and his having died for him as evidence that Christ died for each one of us. In another passage (§616), it cites Paul's affirmation of the death of Christ as an act of love that has redeemed us.

[3:2] The *Catechism* uses this verse to defend the practice of artistically representing images of Jesus Christ as a human being (§476).

[3:6–14] In a section on the role of Abraham in salvation history, the *Catechism* refers to Paul's citation of God's promise to Abraham that he would be the father of many nations (§59; Gen 12:3; 18:17–19; Gal 3:8). It also uses this passage to speak of Christ taking on the burdens of the law (§§578, 580), and it refers to the promise of the Spirit (v. 14; §§693, 705–6).

[3:19–22] This passage appears in sections on the promises given to Abraham and their fulfillment in Christ (§§706, 708), and on the ways in which the Mosaic law prepared for the new law, while acknowledging both strengths and weaknesses in the law of Moses (§1963).

[3:23–29] The *Catechism* cites Paul's expression of the law as a temporary "pedagogue" (v. 24) to help people move in the direction of Christ (§708; cf. §582). Paul's famous expression of the unity the baptized find in Christ (vv. 27–28) is also used (§791), as well as various references to the nature of baptism into Christ and being "clothed" anew in Christ (§§1227, 1243). In a section on the sacrament of reconciliation, the *Catechism* cites verse 27 as showing why sin should play no role in the lives of those who "put on Christ" (§1425). Later, while discussing the sixth commandment, the *Catechism* uses the same verse 27 to explain that those who have been clothed with Christ, the one true chaste person, are called to chastity (§2348).

[4:4–5] The *Catechism* cites this passage (especially v. 4) several times (§§422, 484, 488) in relation to Mary's special role in salvation history, bearing the Word made flesh. Another passage (§702) uses the expression "fullness of time" to recall the divinely appointed hour at which God's plan for universal salvation would begin, starting with Mary's special role.

[4:5–6] The *Catechism* cites this verse under the topic of belief in the Holy Spirit (§683), the one who empowers us to cry out, *"Abba!* Father!" (§2766). Later, the same verse is used to affirm one of the many titles of the Holy Spirit, the "Spirit of adoption" (§§693, 742).

[4:19] The *Catechism* uses this verse to explain the nativity of Jesus, "Only when Christ is formed in us will the mystery of Christmas be fulfilled in us" (§526). This verse is also used to emphasize that we must continually strive to be like Christ until we are "formed" in him (§793).

[4:26] The *Catechism* references this verse in a section on various symbols of the Church—the Church as Jerusalem "above" and "our mother" (§757).

[5:1–6] The *Catechism* addresses at length the question of Christian freedom, and unsurprisingly, this passage from Galatians is also featured (§§1739–48). Elsewhere (§578), Galatians 5:3 is used to bolster a citation from the Letter of James (Jas 2:10) on accomplishing the whole of the law. Verse 6 is also cited to affirm that faith and love go together (§1814; also §162).

[5:16–21] In a section on the ninth commandment, the *Catechism* refers to Paul's warning against "sins of the flesh" that are against the Spirit (§2515). Quoting verses 19–21, the *Catechism* mentions that Paul had identified many kinds of sin that were evident of life according to the "flesh" (§1852). The *Catechism* also cites the seriousness of the sin of idolatry to which Paul refers in verse 20 (§2114).

[5:22–26] The *Catechism* cites the Pauline expression of crucifying the flesh and its desires (v. 24) in order to be better led by the Spirit (§2543, 2555; cf. also §§2516, 2842, 2848). Verses 22–23 are referenced for the "fruit of the Spirit" that comes from life in Christ (§§736, 1695).

[6:1–10] The *Catechism* applies the notion of bearing one another's burdens (v. 2) to the challenges of married life (§1642). It also opens the section on the Church as "mother and teacher" (§2030) with the Pauline expression of "the law of Christ" (v. 2), which the Church is obliged to teach.

[6:11–18] The Pauline expression "new creation" (v. 15) in this passage is connected to the new life Christians receive through baptism (§1214).

Appendix III

GALATIANS IN THE LITURGICAL AND SPIRITUAL LIFE OF THE CHURCH

A lectionary is an official book of liturgical readings from the Bible chosen in accordance with related themes that coincide with celebrations in the liturgical year or to give broad exposure to the Scriptures. Denominations that use lectionaries do so to ensure a wide choice of Scriptures for worship services. On the one hand, preachers need not be concerned about choosing a passage or a theme. On the other hand, it involves editing the readings that sometimes prevent their wider context from being used.

The Roman Catholic lectionary provided the basis for the Revised Common Lectionary (1994) now used by several denominations, such as Episcopalians and Lutherans. The present Roman Catholic lectionary (2002) follows the practice of using semicontinuous readings from many books of the Bible. The design of the lectionary is simple. Sunday readings are divided into a three-year cycle with each year devoted to one Synoptic Gospel (Matthew, Mark, or Luke). John is read every year, especially in the seasons of Lent and Easter, and to some extent at Christmas. The weekday cycle is divided into two alternating years, odd-numbered (Year I) and even-numbered (Year II). On Sundays, when there are always three readings and a psalm response after the first reading, the theme of the second reading does not always match that of the first reading and the Gospel of the day. When excerpts from the Pauline letters are read, they form this middle reading.

For Sundays, Galatians is employed in this format during liturgical year C (the Year of Luke). Short excerpts from almost all of the six chapters are read on consecutive Sundays of Ordinary Time, as follows:

Ninth Sunday	Galatians 1:1–2, 6–10
Tenth Sunday	Galatians 1:11–19
Eleventh Sunday	Galatians 2:16, 19–21
Twelfth Sunday	Galatians 3:26–29

| Thirteenth Sunday | Galatians 5:1, 13–18 |
| Fourteenth Sunday | Galatians 6:14–18 |

On Pentecost Sunday of Year B (the Year of Mark), the lectionary uses Galatians 5:16–25 as the second reading, with clear reference to the contrast between life lived according to the "flesh" and that according to the "Spirit."

Every year on January 1, the Solemnity of Mary the Mother of God, the lectionary uses Galatians 4:4–7 as the second reading, obviously in deference to the incarnation, found in the subtle reference to Jesus Christ being "born of a woman" (cf. also *VD* 11).

For the weekday cycle, Galatians is read in semicontinuous sequence during the twenty-seventh and twenty-eighth weeks of Year II, in the following order:

Twenty-Seventh Week:

Monday	Galatians 1:6–12
Tuesday	Galatians 1:13–24
Wednesday	Galatians 2:1–2, 7–14
Thursday	Galatians 3:1–5
Friday	Galatians 3:7–14
Saturday	Galatians 3:22–29

Twenty-Eighth Week:

Monday	Galatians 4:22–24, 26–27, 31—5:1
Tuesday	Galatians 5:1–6
Wednesday	Galatians 5:18–25

For preachers, trying to explain texts that are cited only partially outside the context of the letter can be challenging. It is difficult to avoid distorting the text. Note, too, that the citations are sometimes edited, with some sections excised for the sake of brevity or to avoid extraneous themes. It is not easy to explain sufficiently the complexities of Paul's text without getting bogged down in too many details.[1]

Other specific passages from Galatians in the lectionary include the following:

2:19–20. The lectionary uses this passage on the memorial (July 23) of Saint Bridget of Sweden (1302/3–73), a widow with eight children, and a mystic who was known for her visions and piety.

3:26–28. This passage on the new identity achieved by baptism is recommended for ceremonies of Christian initiation, apart from the Easter Vigil, including rites of baptizing infants.

4:4–7. This passage is recommended for the Feast of the Most Holy Name of Mary (Sept. 12), which is ironic, given that she is not named. It is also a recommended reading for Christian initiation for the obvious connection of becoming God's children and being able to address God with the familiar "*Abba*! Father!"

4:12–19. This passage, which describes Paul's illness and the Galatians' assistance, is a possible reading for anointing the sick.

5:16–21, 22–26. The lectionary recommends 5:17–26 in the following Votive Masses (i.e., Masses for special intentions): for country, city, or those in public office, or for war or civil disturbance. This choice likely reflects the contrast between good and evil of which civil officials should be mindful in fulfilling their duties of leadership. Galatians 5:16–25 is a recommended reading for rites of the sacrament of confirmation, likely because of the contrast of ethical behaviors to be aware of as one confirms their commitment to the Christian faith.

6:14–18. This passage, in which Paul mentions the marks (*stigmata*) of suffering that he himself has, is used on the Feast of Saint Francis of Assisi (October 4), a universally admired saint whose gentleness, sensitivity to creation, and pacifistic teachings make him a modern favorite. He is also known for receiving the stigmata of Christ, the marks of the crucifixion, on his own body, a sign of his intense piety.

THE LITURGY OF THE HOURS

The Liturgy of the Hours is also known as the Divine Office of the Work of God (Lat. *Opus Dei*, "work of God"). It constitutes the official prayer of the Church, a collection of hymns, readings, and prayers. It grew out of a monastic type of prayer that is entirely based upon the Bible. There is a four-week cycle of psalms to be prayed at specific hours marking the day. It is a way to recall the obligation to give thanks to God for the gift of each precious day.

The five principal divisions of the Office are the Office of Readings, Morning Prayer, Midday Prayer (subdivided into midmorning, midday, and midafternoon), Evening Prayer, and Night Prayer. Each hour of the day includes biblical readings and prayers, and throughout the month-long cycle, virtually all the psalms are prayed. The Office of Readings includes biblical readings and others from the Christian tradition (such as patristic quotations, medieval commentaries, writings of various saints, or passages from magisterial documents). Because of their importance, certain biblical passages appear every day for designated hours, such as the canticles from Luke's Gospel: the Prayer of Zechariah (Lat. *Benedictus*, Luke 1:68–79) for Morning Prayer; the Magnificat, Mary's Song of Praise (Lat. *Magnificat*, Luke 1:46b–55) for Evening Prayer; and Simeon's Canticle (Luke 2:29–32) for Night Prayer.

Recitation of the Liturgy of the Hours is obligatory for ordained Roman Catholic clergy, but in recent years, some parishes have introduced the practice of morning and evening prayer to invite the laity into this prayerful experience. In monasteries, of course, the monks or religious sisters usually pray (or sing) the Liturgy of the Hours in common, and often all the hours of the day (e.g., midday prayer or prayer in the middle of the night) are included, not simply Morning, Evening, and Night Prayer.

The full Liturgy of the Hours exists in a four-volume set according to the liturgical seasons (Advent–Christmas; Lent–Easter; and Ordinary Time [2 vols.]), but one-volume editions also exist, without the Office of Readings, and require that one flip back and forth to various repeated readings. Some online versions are also available free of charge (or for a modest fee), notably Universalis (http://universalis.com) and iBreviary (http://www.ibreviary.org/en/; as an app for mobile phones and tablets; available in multiple languages and free of charge).

Galatians is a short letter. Its entire text is read sequentially as the NT reading in the Office of Readings from Sunday to Saturday for week five of Ordinary Time in the liturgical year. The table below shows the sequence of readings and the extrabiblical readings that are paired with the excerpts from Galatians, along with a comment to explain how the accompanying texts are linked to the biblical reading.

Sequential Reading of Galatians in the Office of Readings, Week 5 of Ordinary Time			
DAY	**PASSAGE FROM GALATIANS**	**ACCOMPANYING TEXT**	**COMMENT**
Sunday	1:1-12	From an explanation of Paul's letter to the Galatians by Saint Augustine, bishop (*Prefacio* PL 35, 2105-7)	Emphasizes the divine origin of Paul's call and his gospel message (Gal 1:12)
Monday	1:13—2:10	From a short discourse by Saint Bonaventure, bishop (*Prologus: Opera omnia* 5, 201-2)	Emphasizes that knowledge of Jesus Christ permits one to understand all the Scriptures; though various Scriptures are quoted, there is no explicit citation of Galatians
Tuesday	2:11—3:14	From a homily on Genesis by Origen, priest (*Hom.* 8,6,8,9: PG 12, 206-9);	Ties in with Abraham's sacrifice of his son Isaac (Gal 3:6-9)

Continued

GALATIANS

Wednesday	3:15—4:7	From a letter by Saint Ambrose, bishop (*Ep.* 35,4-6, 13: PL 16 [ed. 1845], 1078–79, 1081)	Picks up on the prayerful expression *"Abba"* (Gal 4:6) and being "heirs" of the promise (Gal 4:5-7)
Thursday	4:8-31	From an explanation of Paul's letter to the Galatians by Saint Augustine, bishop (*Nn.* 37, 38: PL 35, 2131-32)	Ties into Paul's call on the Galatians (and elsewhere in his letters) to become like him and be formed in Christ (Gal 4:19)
Friday	5:1-25	From a sermon by Saint Leo the Great, pope (*Sermo in Nativitate Domine* 7,2,6: PL 54, 217–18, 220-21)	Picks up on Paul's contrast of life in the flesh versus life in the Spirit (Gal 5:16-23)
Saturday	5:25—6:18	From a sermon by Blessed Isaac of Stella, abbot (*Sermo* 31L PL 194, 1292-93) on the preeminence of charity	Emphasizes the preeminence of charity and the need to "bear one another's burdens" (Gal 6:2)

Apart from the Office of Readings, Galatians does not get extensive exposure in the Liturgy of the Hours but appears in certain key contexts, as summarized below.

Galatians 1:11–24. Unsurprisingly, given its autobiographical nature, this reading appears in the Office of Readings for the Solemnity of the Conversion of Paul (January 25).

Galatians 2:19b–20. This passage that has so influenced many spiritual writers and mystics throughout Christian history appears as the reading for Friday Morning Prayer every fourth week (Week 4).

Galatians 3:22—4:7. This is an alternate reading for the Office of Readings on feasts of the Blessed Virgin Mary (Liturgy of the Hours, Vol. 3:1620–21; Vol. 4:1634–35).

Galatians 1:15—2:10. This is the first reading of the Office of Readings on the Solemnity of Peter and Paul (June 29). The second reading on this same day is from a sermon of Saint Augustine on Galatians.

Galatians 2:19—3:7, 13–14; 6:14–16. Because of the emphasis on the cross of Christ, this is the first reading in the Office of Readings (Vol. 4) for the Feast of the Exaltation of the Holy Cross (September 14), celebrated by multiple denominations under different names.

LECTIO DIVINA

Lectio divina (Latin for "prayerful reading" of Scripture) is an ancient prayer form also molded in the context of monastic traditions. Its purpose is to promote the use of Scriptures in prayer so that each Christian can become more familiar with them.

There are many possible formats for *lectio divina*, but recent years have shown a resurgence in interest in the Benedictine practice, which includes four main steps.

Lectio: reading a passage, slowly and prayerfully

Oratio: oral prayer, addressing a word to God that reflects your understanding of, and gratitude for, the word

Meditatio: using the imagination to meditate or reflect on the passage, perhaps focusing on a word or phrase that is particularly significant or attractive

Contemplatio: contemplation, remaining quiet in God's presence in appreciation of the gift of this particular word

This ancient practice has made an impact not only on the Catholic practice of praying the Scriptures, but many Protestant groups have begun to encourage the exercise of prayerful reading of Scripture using similar methods. Most important is the goal of growing closer to Scripture as the living word of God. While *lectio divina* developed as a prayer form long after Saint Paul, his use of Scripture (the OT only, of course) in Galatians clearly shows his appreciation of the Bible as the living word of God whose validity is for all time (e.g., his use of Scripture in Gal 4:21–31), something he states explicitly in Romans, where he writes,

> For everything that was written in former days was written for our instruction, so that through perseverance and through the encouragement of the Scriptures we might have hope. (Rom 15:4, au. trans.)

Applying the principles of *lectio divina* can be easy. One can choose to read through the letter section by section, following the divisions (or subdivisions) of this commentary or even one of the available Bible translations. It is ideal not to rush this process, though a session of *lectio* need not be long to be fruitful. Allow Paul's words to sink in deeply, drawing you further into the depth of his love for God, his appreciation of God's word, and his affection for his Galatian communities.[2]

GLOSSARY

This glossary is limited to terms used in Galatians or other technical terms referred to in this commentary.

Abba: Aramaic expression akin to "Dad" used by Jesus, and subsequently by Christians, to address God as Father in a familiar way (Gal 4:6; Rom 8:15; Mark 14:36).

allegory/allegorical: an extended comparison in which each of the elements generally correspond (Gal 4:21–31); a form of biblical interpretation characteristic of some Church fathers that emphasizes such correspondences.

amanuensis (Lat. *a manu*, "by hand"): a scribe or secretary, someone who could read and write professionally; Paul mostly dictated his letters to scribes, who wrote them out and copied them (Rom 16:22).

Ambrosiaster: an anonymous fourth-century CE commentary on all the letters of Saint Paul (except Hebrews, which some ancient authors attributed to Paul); once mistakenly identified with Saint Ambrose, hence the name.

aorist: the simple past tense of a Greek verb (e.g., "did") as distinct from the continuous past ("was doing" or "used to do"), the present perfect ("has done"), or the past perfect ("had done").

apocalyptic: a type of thought or literature that developed in times of persecution and emphasized the contrast between the present world (and its sufferings) and the world to come (and its victory over evil).

apocrypha (Gk. *apokryphos*, "hidden"): refers to books apart from the accepted OT canon for which divine authorship was not accepted (e.g., 1 Esdras [Ezra], 4 Esdras [Ezra], Jubilees, 3 Baruch, Sibylline Oracles), or, similarly, books not included in the NT canon because of doubtful divine authorship (e.g., Gospel of Mary, Gospel of Peter, Gospel of Thomas, Infancy Gospel of Thomas, Gospel of Judas, Acts of Paul and Thecla). Contrary to popular misconception, the Vatican has never hidden these books; they are available in various published editions.

apology/apologetic: defense or defensive; characterizes some forms of ancient rhetorical style, either oral or written.

chiasm/chiastic: a symmetrical arrangement of words, phrases, or ideas, such as *a, b, c, b', a'*.

Christology/christological: a technical expression derived from two Greek terms, *christos* (anointed one) and *logos* (word), that refers to all aspects of the study of Jesus as the Christ or Messiah, including both his human and divine identity.

circumcision: cutting of the foreskin of the male sexual organ; Greeks thought the practice barbaric, but Jews saw it as an essential identification that derived from Abraham's covenant with God (Gen 17:10–12); the agitators in Galatia wished to turn the Galatians to this Jewish practice, which for Paul was contrary to the meaning of the gospel of Jesus Christ and its freedom from the law of Moses.

conscience: the faculty of moral judgment by which a person recognizes the rightness or wrongness of actions.

Council of Jerusalem: a meeting in Jerusalem of early Christian leaders like Peter, Paul, and James the brother of the Lord around 49 to 50 CE, recorded in Acts 15:1–21 and Galatians 2:1–10, to address the implications of preaching the gospel of Jesus Christ to the gentiles.

covenant (Heb. *berith*; Gk. *diathēkē*): a treaty or agreement between God and Israel; the Greek word can also mean "testament" (as in the Latin Vulgate trans. *testamentum*).

Cynic (Gk. *kynikos*, "like a dog"): one of the Hellenistic philosophical trends of Paul's day; it was founded in the fourth century BCE and was related to skepticism; it taught detachment, self-sufficiency, and freedom; its itinerant lifestyle (doglike) of begging led to considerable ridicule.

deliberative rhetoric: also called hortatory rhetoric, a form of argumentation suited to public debates intended to persuade an audience to act in a certain way.

demonstrative rhetoric: also called epideictic rhetoric, a form of argumentation intended to inspire or to please people in order to garner support or maintain common values.

diaspora (lit. "dispersion"): the designation for the dispersal of Jews throughout the world once they were exiled from the Holy Land (sixth century BCE); Paul was a diaspora Jew (Acts 9:11; 21:39; 22:3).

doxology (Gk. *doxa*, "glory"): a prayer of praise to God; Paul sometimes incorporates doxologies in his letters (e.g., Gal 1:5; Rom 11:33–36).

epideictic rhetoric: see demonstrative rhetoric.

Epiphanius: one of the fathers of the Church in the fourth century (ca. 315–403 CE) and bishop of Salamis (Cyprus), known for combatting heresies of that era.

eschatology/eschatological: having to do with the "end times," which can be understood either as still coming or as the final times ushered in by Jesus Christ. Thus, the NT asserts that we are living "in these last days" (Heb 1:2), introduced by the resurrection of Jesus Christ and the sending of the Holy Spirit (Acts 2:17). Still, Christians look forward to a final consummation with the return of Christ.

exile: the experience of the enslavement of the Jews after the first destruction of Jerusalem and the temple by the Babylonians in 587 BCE and lasting until 537 BCE, when the

Persians allowed them to return to rebuild their city; virtually the entire population was forcefully relocated to Babylon.

faith (Gk. *pistis*): (1) in Paul, faith is a complex concept with nuanced meanings depending upon context; it is usually a relational term (from the verb "believe" [Gk. *pisteuō*]) that entails belief in the truth about Jesus as Lord, Messiah, and Son of God, and faithfulness characterized by trust, surrender, and obedience (Gal 2:20; Rom 1:5; 10:8–10); (2) Christ's faithfulness to God (Gal 2:16); (3) confidence or trust in God and God's word (2 Cor 5:7).

flesh (Gk. *sarx*): (1) the body or physical existence (Gal 2:20); (2) corruptible and fallen human nature characterized by sinful inclinations and disordered desires (Gal 5:19–20) and contrasted with the proper inclinations of the Spirit (Gal 5:22–23); (3) what is merely human as in the phrase "flesh and blood" (Gal 1:16); (4) anatomical word for muscle or a body's soft tissue (Luke 24:39).

French school of spirituality: a term used to describe a seventeenth-century Catholic renewal movement in France to respond to the calls of the Council of Trent to reform the Catholic Church; though not formally a "school," several significant holy figures contributed to its tenets, especially Pierre de Bérulle, Jean Eudes, Vincent de Paul, and Jean-Jacques Olier; they often cite Paul's letters in their writings.

gentiles (Heb. *goiim*; Gk. *ethnē* [can also be translated "nations"]): (1) non-Jews; (2) people outside of the covenant relationship with God, that is, pagans; Paul's great insight was that gentiles could belong to God's people, too, without becoming Jews, because of the salvation achieved in Jesus Christ (Eph 3:6).

gospel (Gk. *euanggelion*, "good news," and *euanggelizomai*, "proclaim good news"): (1) the good news of salvation through the death and resurrection of Jesus Christ, which calls for a response of faith and repentance; (2) the Christian message in its entirety. A key concept in Paul's letters (Gal 1:7–9); later the word *Gospel* (capitalized) came to refer to one of the four canonical narratives of the life of Jesus in the NT.

grace (Gk. *charis*): (1) an attitude of favor, generosity, or magnanimity, especially on the part of God; (2) a freely given energy from God that helps to direct one's life; (3) a greeting used in Pauline letters, often accompanied by "peace" or "mercy" (Gal 1:3; 6:16, 18).

Greco-Roman: the political and cultural world of Paul and his churches, combining both Greek and Roman influences.

Hellenistic: the Greek cultural influence of Paul's world; it began with Alexander the Great of Macedon (356–323 BCE), who promoted Greek culture throughout the ancient world.

house church: a modern sociological term to describe the nature of early Christian communities, which gathered for worship and fellowship, not in church buildings but in private homes.

incarnation (Lat. *incarnatio*, "enfleshment"): a concept used for the doctrine of God taking on flesh, becoming human and being born like all human beings; although not a major concept in Paul's letters, Galatians 4:4 hints at it (cf. also Phil 2:7).

Josephus: Flavius Josephus, born Yosef ben Mattatyahu (ca. 37–100 CE), was an aristocratic, well-educated Jew who was close to certain Roman emperors (the Flavians) and became a Jewish-Roman historian. His extant writings provide important background on the history of the Jews and pertinent cultural and historical information for Jewish and Roman figures, customs, and events in the NT period.

judicial rhetoric: also called forensic, the argumentative style in courts of law used to prosecute or defend someone.

justification/justify (Gk. *dikaiosynē/dikaiōsis/dikaioō*): a forensic term meaning to be declared or made righteous in God's eyes; rectitude; see also righteous/righteousness below; most Protestants identify this concept as the key theological element in Paul's thought, while Catholics see it as one of several important concepts related to God's offer of salvation through Jesus Christ.

Kephas (Gk. *Cephas*): Aramaic for "rock"; nickname of Simon Peter (Gal 1:18; 2:9, 11) whom Jesus surnamed the "Rock" on whom he would build the Church (Matt 16:18).

law of Moses (Mosaic law): the commandments or precepts of God given to Moses on Mount Sinai (Exod 19—20) and preserved in the Pentateuch, the first five books of the Bible; also called torah (Heb. "instruction").

Lord (Gk. *kyrios*): a christological title in the NT referring to Jesus Christ's divine status as exalted "Lord of the universe"; in Greek secular usage, it could be an address of a man as "sir" or "master"; in the LXX, the word translates the Hebrew *adonai* as a circumlocution for the name of God (Heb. *YHWH*), which was not supposed to be pronounced. "Lord" is Paul's favorite title for Jesus Christ.

LXX: see Septuagint.

Messiah/messianic (Heb. *mashiach*, "anointed"; Gk. *christos*): a late OT concept referring to the Jewish expectation of God's anointed one who was to come and rescue Israel from its enemies; early Christians saw in Jesus a fulfillment of this hope, albeit in a totally unexpected way as a humble, suffering servant.

monotheism (Gk. *monos theos*, "a single god"): belief in one God; Judaism, Christianity, and Islam are the world's principal monotheistic religions.

nomism: a scholarly term for legalism, reducing the law (of Moses) to a set of rigid moral codes.

ostraca (Gk. *ostrakon*, "shell, sherd"): pottery fragments from antiquity that have small amounts of writing in various languages on them from letters, lists, receipts, notes, school exercises, and the like; an important source of archaeological information on the Bible.

paraenesis/paraenetic: ethical or moral instruction or exhortation; most of Paul's letters contain such passages (e.g., Gal 5:16–26).

pedagogue: a slave or servant who accompanied boys to their classes and who helped them learn; Paul uses the term metaphorically for the law (Gal 3:25).

Philo of Alexandria: an influential Jewish philosopher, political leader, and prolific author (ca. 20 BCE–50 CE) in Alexandria, Egypt; his extensive writings testify to the influence of Hellenistic thought on Jews living in the diaspora in NT times; they also influenced many Church fathers, especially regarding his allegorical interpretations of the OT.

pneumatology (Gk. *pneuma* + *logos*, "study of the Spirit"): the analysis of the role of the Holy Spirit in one's theology; the notion of the Spirit comes from the Hebrew word (*ruach*) and the Greek word (*pneuma*) meaning (1) breath; (2) the seat of interiority— and by extension, spirituality—in human beings; or (3) God's Spirit or the "breath" of God. The ancients recognized the relationship between breath and life (Gen 1:30; 2:7) and applied it as well to the gift of spiritual life.

redeem/redemption (Gk. *exagorazō*, "buy back"): often used of buying back or ransoming slaves; used figuratively of Jesus's salvific action through the cross and resurrection of redeeming humanity from the burden of the law and the effects of sin (Gal 3:13; 4:5).

revelation (Gk. *apokalypsis*, "unveiling"): an event or an insight that comes about by God's action; for Paul, it may indicate something akin to a mystical experience (Gal 1:12; 2:2).

rhetoric: the science and art of persuasive oratory defined by the philosopher Aristotle (394– 322 BCE) and his successors; classified into three main categories: judicial, demonstrative, and deliberative (see above).

righteous/righteousness (Gk. *dikaiosynē/dikaiōsis/dikaioō*): (1) a right relationship with God and fellow human beings; (2) as a quality of God, it means being accepted as living in proper relationship with God; also see justification/justify above.

Septuagint (abbreviated LXX from Latin for "70"): Greek translation of the Hebrew Bible for the Jews of the diaspora, dating from the third to second century BCE, so called because of the tradition that it was the work of seventy scholars working independently to produce a faithful translation; often quoted or alluded to in the NT, it was the Bible used by Greek-speaking Jews and Christians, including Paul.

sin (Gk. *hamartia*, "failure, error, miss the mark"): transgression of God's law; Paul sees it as a corrupting and persuasive evil power in human life (Gal 2:17; 3:22)—thus, Sin—but at times views such transgressions collectively as "sins" (Gal 1:4).

spirit (Gk. *pneuma*): (1) an interior or ethereal aspect of human existence in contrast to the "flesh"; (2) the Holy Spirit.

stigmata: (1) marks or brands on the bodies of slaves attesting to their status as slaves and their owner (Gal 6:17); (2) the five marks of the crucified body of Jesus (hands, feet, side) that some mystics throughout the history of spirituality have received.

Stoic: one of the common Hellenistic philosophical schools of Paul's day; founded in Athens by the philosopher Zeno (ca. 336–263 BCE), Stoicism was a reaction against Epicurean philosophy; it emphasized self-control, a virtuous life, and a calm approach to life's challenges; some aspects of this philosophy were harmonious with Christian values promoted by Paul (cf. Acts 17:18).

testament (Gk. *diathēkē*): (1) a person's will; (2) designation for a collection of the sacred books (OT and NT).

torah (Heb. "instruction" or "teaching"): (1) God's instructions and commandments contained in the law of Moses; (2) the canonical designation for the first five books of the Bible, also called the Pentateuch.

Trinity/trinitarian: the Christian belief of three persons in one God; the seeds of this doctrine are found in Paul's letters, even if the full understanding of this mystery would take centuries for the Church to develop.

Vatican Council II: the twenty-first ecumenical Church council (1962–65) that dramatically changed the life of the Catholic Church in the middle of the twentieth century, and that led to ecumenism, modern Catholic biblical studies, liturgy in the vernacular, and so on. Its sixteen authoritative documents still guide the life of the Catholic Church.

Vulgate (Lat. "common"): Latin translation of the entire Bible, often attributed to Saint Jerome (ca. 340–420)—disputed by some scholars—but done on the basis of older Latin editions and based on the original Hebrew and Greek texts; later it became the principal version of the Bible for the Roman Catholic Church; today a revised "New Vulgate" (*Nova Vulgata*) is the primary reference for Catholic translations of the Bible used in the liturgy.

NOTES

PREFACE

1. For more on the history and background of the document, see Ronald D. Witherup, *Scripture*: Dei Verbum, Rediscovering Vatican II series (Mahwah, NJ: Paulist, 2006); for a commentary, see Ronald D. Witherup, *The Word of God at Vatican II: Exploring* Dei Verbum (Collegeville, MN: Liturgical Press, 2014).

1. THE GREETING (1:1–5)

1. Many Bible translations capitalize the word *gentile* (NRSV, NABRE), but more recently scholars have preferred the word in lower case. The reason is that, in contrast to the word *Jew*, the word *gentile* does not connote an ethnic identity but is a broad nonethnic category for non-Jews.

2. Paul's Jewish name Saul is the same as the first king of Israel (1 Sam 9:15; 10:1), who was also from the tribe of Benjamin (Phil 3:5). Paul is proud of this heritage, and there is no reason to doubt that he continued to use his Jewish name in such circles. Among his gentile converts, he was known as Paul, and all his letters reflect this usage. See the expression, "Saul, also known as Paul" (Acts 13:9).

3. Other texts reflect subtler references to resurrection (or new life): 2:19–21; 3:19–21; 5:24–25; 6:8; 6:14–15. See Andrew Boakye, *Death and Life: Resurrection, Restoration, and Rectification in Paul's Letter to the Galatians* (Eugene, OR: Pickwick, 2017). I am grateful to Prof. Michael Gorman for this reference.

4. The NRSV translates the expression "all the members of God's family." The Greek expression *adelphoi* ("brothers") in this context could legitimately be translated "brothers and sisters" to be more inclusive, as the NABRE footnote indicates.

5. A similarly vague expression, "the brothers who are with me," occurs at the end of Philippians (4:21). Note that a certain "Crescens" is described as having left Paul and gone to Galatia (2 Tim 4:10).

6. See 1 Cor 1:1; 2 Cor 1:1; Phil 1:1; Col 1:1; 1 Thess 1:1; 2 Thess 1:1.

7. The concept of grace is more complex than the greeting might imply. Paul's understanding of grace is like a spiritual power of God, a divine graciousness or generosity, operative in the universe, a hidden but powerful energy that mysteriously directs the cosmos

through the action of the Holy Spirit. It figures prominently in Paul's letters and is related to the gifts (*charismata*) of the Holy Spirit (e.g., Rom 5:15, 20; 1 Cor 15:10; 2 Cor 4:15). See *CCC* §1996–2005 for a contemporary Christian understanding of grace.

8. Some manuscripts read "God and Father of our Lord Jesus Christ." Most scholars judge this form to be a scribal change from Paul's traditional formula to emphasize the christological dimension of the text, but note that this alternative form of the expression occurs elsewhere in Paul's letters (Rom 15:6; 2 Cor 1:3; Eph 1:3).

9. Elsewhere in Galatians (3:13; 4:5), Paul uses the word *exagorazō* for Christ's redemptive act, with the sense of redeeming or buying back humanity from slavery.

10. Later, Paul emphasizes the personal dimension of this notion: Jesus gave himself up "for me" (Gal 2:20).

11. Cf. Rom 1:25; 9:5; 11:33–36; 16:27; Phil 4:20; 1 Thess 3:11–13; Eph 3:14–21; 1 Tim 1:17; 6:16; 2 Tim 4:18.

2. FIDELITY TO THE GOSPEL (1:6–10)

1. Rom 1:8–15; 1 Cor 1:4–9; 2 Cor 1:3–7; 1 Thess 1:2–10; Phlm 4–6, etc. At times, the thanksgiving section appears in other places in the body of the letter or is mingled with prayer sections (1 Thess 2:13–16). The Letter to Titus also lacks a formal thanksgiving, although it is less polemical than Galatians.

2. For this reason, I have chosen to use the term *agitators* in this commentary.

3. NET and NAS translate the word "distort." Perhaps Paul subtly faults both those who have led the Galatians astray and the Galatians themselves by using Greek terms in parallel verses that both begin with the same preposition *meta* ("from"): forsaking or abandoning (*metatithēmi*) and perverting or distorting (*metastrephō*). Both groups are turning from the truth.

4. Paul uses the noun "gospel" (*euaggelion*) exclusively in the singular; the "good news" or "glad tidings" is a singular event, or more correctly, rooted in a singular person, Jesus Christ.

3. PAUL'S DEFENSE OF THE GOSPEL
AND HIS AUTHORITY (1:11–2:21)

1. Note that this pattern of the negative assertions followed by a positive one mirrors what Paul had said about the divine origin of his message in 1:1.

2. 1:12; 2:19, 20; 4:12; 5:2, 10, 11; 6:17.

3. Despite the differences in details, note that both Acts and Galatians indicate that Damascus was the locale where Paul had his life-changing experience of the risen Lord.

4. This is the suggestion of N.T. Wright, "Paul, Arabia, and Elijah (Galatians 1:17)," *JBL* 115 (1996): 683–92. Elijah's prophetic identity, well-known zeal, and willingness to confront false prophets fit well with Paul's own self-identity.

5. "Cephas" is the Greek form of this Aramaic name and is sometimes retained in translation. In whatever the language—Aramaic, Greek, Latin—the pun "rock" remains.

6. The notion that Paul, a major persecutor, would not have been known "by sight" (*tō prosōpō*) in Jerusalem seems incongruous, if in fact he had studied in Jerusalem under Gamaliel (Acts 22:3) and had sought permission from the high priest there to hunt down Christ believers in Damascus (Acts 9:1–2, "any who belonged to the Way"). Perhaps Paul means he was not known as a Christ believer, what became known as "Christians" (Acts 11:26; 26:28).

7. Note that James is listed first here. This hints at his precedence at this point, having already succeeded Peter as the main leader of the mother church.

8. Note that Paul mentions himself first, before Barnabas (grammatically bad English!). Historically, Paul was the understudy of Barnabas at the beginning (Acts 9:27; 11:22–26) when they both were "apostles" for the church in Antioch. Already evident, though, are tensions between them, to which Paul will allude (Gal 2:13), and which ultimately led to a parting of the ways (Acts 15:39).

9. Keep in mind that Paul's letters would likely have been orally read in his churches, as most people could not read.

10. Because the vocabulary of justification has so much "baggage" to it, some might suggest using "rectification." I have nonetheless retained the traditional language familiar to most readers.

11. The "Joint Declaration on the Doctrine of Justification" is available at http://www.vatican.va/roman_curia/pontifical_councils/chrstuni/documents/rc_pc_chrstuni_doc_31101999_cath-luth-joint-declaration_en.html. See R. D. Witherup, "Bringing an Ecumenical Milestone out of the Shadows," *Intersections* 30 (2009): 5–7.

4. FAITH AND FREEDOM IN CHRIST (3:1–4:31)

1. The NJB's translation, "announced the future gospel to Abraham," makes this even more explicit.

2. Throughout this section of the letter, Paul's citations from the OT are not random; he quotes related texts because of certain key "catchwords" that recur in one form or another in the texts chosen from the LXX.

3. Thus, the NRSV reads, "I give an example from daily life" (also NIV, NET) and the REB says, "Let me give you an illustration." These expressions indicate a neutral stance on Paul's part, but he may be trying to contrast more sharply a divine viewpoint with his own (temporarily) human view.

4. Calvin (p. 102) interprets the mediator to be Christ rather than Moses.

5. Some interpreters (Barclay, 32–33) have seen in Paul's phrase a reversal of a Jewish morning prayer prayed by men that expressed, "Blessed is God who has not made me a

gentile…a slave…or a woman." This prayer is attested among various rabbis, but the date of its precise origin is uncertain. Modern Jews have generally abandoned this prayer or changed it into a positive one of being blessed for having been created "an Israelite, a free person, and a human being" (see *JANT*, 379).

6. A related term for Paul is "slave of God" (Titus 1:1; Rom 6:22). Whether for Christ or for God his Father, becoming a "slave" means voluntarily exercising humble service for others.

7. See Cohen, *JANT*, 339.

8. See Joseph A. Fitzmyer, "Pauline Theology," *NJBC* §82:49–53.

9. The underlying Greek is not identical in these passages, but the basic meaning is "in the fulness of time."

10. See Gal 4:4.

11. See Col 2:9.

12. See Gal 4:4; Heb 10:5.

13. See Luke 1:26–27.

14. *Lumen Gentium* 56; also 61.

15. Verse 17 in the Greek is a bit obscure, as witnessed by the many different translations (NRSV, NJB, etc.). Paul plays off the word "zealously court" (*zēloō* "desire" or "show zeal for") and docs explicitly mention himself and his colleagues, but the sense is that their courting of the Galatians will simultaneously win the agitators disciples and take them away from Paul.

16. Some manuscripts have the diminutive form, *teknia*.

17. The allegory could properly be termed the allegory of "the two women," but because Paul's main point concerns the sons of the two women and the notions of sonship, heirs, and promise, I prefer to consider it an allegory of Abraham's two sons. The neuter plural participle *allēgoroumena* could support this interpretation.

18. This is not a minor point since otherwise it would be possible to use Galatians improperly to oppose Judaism and Christianity. Paul is a Jew involved in an intra-Jewish-Christian debate with ramifications for the gentile believers. Paul shows in Romans 9—11 that he struggles to explain just how God's salvation will work for his own people the Jews if they do not accept Jesus as the Christ. In the end he surrenders in prayer to God's grace (Rom 11:30–36).

5. EXHORTATION TO CHRISTIAN LIVING (5:1–6:10)

1. The force of the dative expression "for freedom" (*tē eleutheria*) is likely purpose, rather than instrumental ("by").

2. There is wide diversity in the translations of this verse (cf. NRSV, NABRE, NIV, NJB, NET), but the sense is the same: choosing circumcision and the law will cut off the Galatians from Christ.

3. The aorist tense of the verb here indicates that the hindrance has definitively happened. Perhaps that is why Paul is unsure if his letter is going to have its desired effect (4:11, 20).

4. While there is little evidence that the God fearers constituted a formal institution in Judaism in Paul's day, certain gentiles clearly were attracted to Judaism but hesitated when they were required to undergo circumcision to complete the conversion.

5. See, for example, other vice and virtue lists in Rom 1:28–31; 1 Cor 5:9–11; Phil 4:8; 1 Tim 3:2–3.

6. Note that Paul connects wicked deeds with loss of the kingdom of God in 1 Cor 6:9–10.

7. The normal Greek verb "walk" is *peripateō*, but here Paul uses *stoicheō* (see also 6:16), a military term with the nuance of "marching in step with" or "following." Perhaps Paul is subtly alluding to the Galatians having once followed the "elements of the world" (*stoicheia*, 4:3, 9), now calling them to follow the Spirit instead (see de Boer, 372).

6. THE CLOSING (6:11–18)

1. Some familiar aspects of Paul's closings are absent in this letter, such as travel plans (Rom 15:22–25; 1 Cor 16:5–9), mention of associates who are with him or being sent by him (1 Cor 16:10–12; Col 4:7–9; Phlm 23), the "holy kiss" or special greeting of Paul's communities (1 Thess 5:26; Rom 16:16; 1 Cor 16:20; 2 Cor 13:12), or request for prayer (1 Thess 5:25; Rom 15:30; Phlm 22). Perhaps Paul feels the tone of his letter does not warrant including these familiar elements.

2. See the authoritative study of Steve Reece, *Paul's Large Letters: Paul's Autographic Subscriptions in the Light of Ancient Epistolary Conventions*, LNTS 561 (London: Bloomsbury T&T Clark, 2017).

3. Paul uses the expression in verbal or nominal form more than fifty times in the undisputed letters. Many occurrences are in Second Corinthians where Paul is engaged in defending his apostleship (e.g., 2 Cor 10—12).

4. In 5:6, Paul uses a form of the word (*energeō*) related to "works" (*ergōn*), also used in 3:5 in the context of God, through the Spirit, allowing the Galatians to work mighty deeds. Faith is anything but a passive reality; faith calls one to action.

5. Note that all three important concepts—grace, mercy, and peace—also occur in 1 Tim 1:2; 2 Tim 1:2; and 2 John 1:3 in opening greetings, and in that order. It is perhaps a more elaborate prayerful blessing than Paul (in the undisputed letters) usually gives. The Letter of Jude uses another expression in which mercy is cited first: "mercy, peace, and love" (1:2).

6. Note that the "Amen" here comes at the end of the letter and parallels, in a fashion, the unusual Amen at the end of the greeting (1:5). They frame the entire letter in a prayerful context—the spirit in which Paul wrote the letter in the hopes that it would change the Galatians' hearts.

7. Is it accidental that Paul uses this terminology in the conclusion only in Galatians and Second Corinthians, the two communities with whom he had the most tempestuous relationship?

AFTERWORD

1. One of the best contemporary succinct summaries of Paul's theology from a Catholic viewpoint remains Joseph A. Fitzmyer's article in the *NJBC*, §82.

2. Robert Farrar Capon, *The Fingerprints of God* (Grand Rapids, MI: Eerdmans, 2000), 58.

APPENDIX III: GALATIANS IN THE LITURGICAL AND SPIRITUAL LIFE OF THE CHURCH

1. For some practical advice on preaching from Paul's letters, see Frank J. Matera, *Strategies for Preaching Paul* (Collegeville, MN: Liturgical Press, 2001).

2. Little Rock Scripture has a useful series of short publications on *lectio divina* of many passages of the Bible, called Alive in the Word. See, for example, Ronald D. Witherup, *Paul, Proclaiming Christ Crucified*, Alive in the Word/A Cloud of Witnesses (Collegeville, MN: Liturgical Press, 2016).

BIBLIOGRAPHY

COMMENTARIES FROM THE EARLIER HISTORY OF INTERPRETATION

Bray, Gerald L., trans. and ed. *Commentaries on Galatians–Philemon by Ambrosiaster*. Ancient Christian Texts. Downers Grove, IL: IVP Academic, 2009. An accessible translation for this early commentary. Galatians is treated on pp. 1–34.

Calvin, John. *Commentaries on the Epistles of Paul to the Galatians and Ephesians*. Translated by William Pringle. Grand Rapids: Eerdmans, 1948. A classic from the Reformed tradition. Galatians is treated on pp. 13–188.

Cooper, Steven Andrew. *Marius Victorinus' Commentary on Galatians*. OECS. New York: Oxford University Press, 2005.

Edwards, Mark J., ed. *Galatians, Ephesians, Philippians*. ACCS. New Testament, vol. 8. Downers Grove, IL: InterVarsity Press, 1999. Part of an ecumenical series, this volume provides an excellent compilation of quotations from patristic authors on each major passage of three letters of Paul. Galatians is treated on pp. 1–100.

Jerome. *Jerome's Commentary on Galatians*. Translated by Andrew Cain. Washington: Catholic University of America Press, 2010. Other versions are also found online.

John Chrysostom. *Homilies on Galatians*. Translated by Philip Schaff. Nicene and Post-Nicene Fathers of the Christian Church 1, vol. 13. Edinburgh: T & T Clark, 1819–93. Also available online (http://www.newadvent.org/fathers/2310.htm) and in an oral reading of the commentary through LibriVox.org (2011).

Levy, Ian Christopher, trans. and ed. *The Letter to the Galatians*. The Bible in Medieval Tradition. Grand Rapids: Eerdmans, 2011. A helpful collection of citations from medieval commentators on Galatians.

Luther, Martin. *Commentary on Galatians*. Translated by Erasmus Middleton. Grand Rapids: Kregel Classics, 1979. One of the great Protestant commentaries on Galatians, obviously with an emphasis on the letter's teaching about justification by faith.

Plumer, Eric. *Augustine's Commentary on Galatians: Introduction, Text, Translation, and Notes*. OECS. New York: Oxford University Press, 2003. A very good edition of this classic commentary by Saint Augustine, with important introductory essays and the Latin text reproduced on pages opposite the excellent English translation.

Thomas Aquinas. *Commentaries on St. Paul's Epistles to Timothy, Titus, and Philemon*. Translated by Chrysostom Baer. South Bend, IN: St. Augustine, 2007.

MODERN SCHOLARLY COMMENTARIES

Betz, Hans Dieter. *Galatians: A Commentary on Paul's Letter to the Churches in Galatia*. Hermeneia. Philadelphia: Fortress, 1979. A technical commentary that broke new ground by paying close attention to the rhetoric of Galatians.

Bruce, F. F. *The Epistle to the Galatians: A Commentary on the Greek Text*. NIGTC. Grand Rapids: Eerdmans, 1982. A conservative Protestant commentary by an astute interpreter who expounds the Greek text well.

Das, A. Andrew. *Galatians*. ConcC. St. Louis: Concordia, 2014. An extensive commentary done mostly from a Lutheran perspective.

de Boer, Martinus. *Galatians: A Commentary*. NTL. Louisville, KY: Westminster John Knox, 2011. An excellent commentary on the Greek text, with many detailed excurses on disputed or problematic passages.

deSilva, David A. *The Letter to the Galatians*. NICNT. Grand Rapids: Eerdmans, 2018. A thorough exegesis and interpretation of the Greek text.

Dunn, James D. G. *Galatians*. BNTC. London: Black, 1993. Very readable commentary with pithy insights and a flair for making the obscure understandable.

Keener, Craig S. *Galatians: A Commentary*. Grand Rapids: Baker Academic, 2019. A formidable, comprehensive commentary by a prolific Protestant author.

Longenecker, Richard N. *Galatians*. WBC 41. Dallas: Word Books, 1990. A thorough technical commentary on the letter from the Evangelical tradition.

Martyn, J. Louis. *Galatians: A New Translation with Introduction and Commentary*. AB 33A. New York: Doubleday, 1997. A detailed scholarly analysis of Galatians filled with many informative side comments as well as a rich exposition of the Greek text.

Matera, Frank J. *Galatians*. SP 9. Collegeville, MN: Liturgical, 1992. A thorough, eminently readable Catholic commentary.

Moo, Douglas J. *Galatians*. BECNT. Grand Rapids: Baker Academic, 2013. A thorough and judicious commentary on the Greek text from an Evangelical perspective.

Riches, John. *Galatians through the Centuries*. BBC. Malden, MA: Blackwell, 2008. A unique commentary that provides a fascinating overview of how individual passages from Galatians have been interpreted through history.

MODERN ACCESSIBLE SCHOLARLY COMMENTARIES

Bedford, Nancy Elizabeth. *Galatians*. Belief. Louisville, KY: Westminster John Knox, 2016. An explicitly theological commentary by a systematic theologian.

Brown, Raymond E. "Letter to the Galatians." In *An Introduction to the New Testament*, 467–82. ABRL. New York: Doubleday, 1998. A succinct but incisive explanation of Galatians, with helpful bibliography. An even shorter version, without notes and bibliography, is found in *An Introduction to the New Testament: The Abridged Edition*, edited by Marion L. Soards, 168–73. AYBRL. New Haven, CT: Yale University Press, 2016.

Byrne, Brendan. *Galatians and Romans*. Collegeville, MN: Liturgical Press, 2010, 1–51. A brief, popular, and insightful exposition of Galatians that can be used in conjunction with a *Study Guide on Galatians and Romans* by Catherine Upchurch and Clifford M. Yeary, published by Little Rock Scripture Study and available through Liturgical Press.

Cousar, Charles B. *Galatians*. Interpretation Commentaries. Atlanta: John Knox, 1982. An easy-to-read commentary that is part of a series intended primarily as an aid to preachers.

Fitzmyer, Joseph A. "The Letter to the Galatians." In *The New Jerome Biblical Commentary*, edited by Raymond E. Brown, et al., §47. Englewood Cliffs, NJ: Prentice-Hall, 1990. A brief yet technical analysis focusing on each verse of the letter.

Hays, Richard B. "Galatians." In *NIB* 11:181–348. A masterful treatment by an outstanding Pauline scholar with sensitivity to pastoral application.

Oakes, Peter A. *Galatians*. Paideia. Grand Rapids: Baker Academic, 2015. A creative commentary in this series that expounds the interpretation of the letter in its cultural, literary, and theological dimensions.

Soards, Marion L., and Darrell J. Pursiful. *Galatians*. SHBC 26a. Macon, GA: Smyth & Helwys, 2015. A good modern commentary filled with illustrations and sidebars, which tries to relate the text to modern contexts; comes with an interactive CD.

Vanhoye, Cardinal Albert, and Peter S. Williamson. *Galatians*. Catholic Commentary on Sacred Scripture. Grand Rapids: Baker Academic, 2019. A very good commentary translated from the original Italian and modified to fit the design of the commentary series.

POPULAR COMMENTARIES

Barclay, William. *The Letter to the Galatians*. Philadelphia: Westminster Press, 1956; rev. ed. 1976. A popular, insightful, pastoral commentary, to be used by checking exegesis against more recent scholarly commentaries.

Cohen, Shaye J. D. "The Letter of Paul to the Galatians." In *The Jewish Annotated New Testament*, edited by Amy-Jill Levine and Marc Zvi Brettler, 2:373–87. New York: Oxford University Press, 2017. The value of this exposition is its Jewish perspective, with detailed and informative notes to the NRSV translation of Galatians.

Gundry, Robert H. *Commentary on Galatians*. Grand Rapids: Baker Academic, 2011. An e-version of a small commentary originally published in 2010, this is a handy, down-to-earth commentary by an Evangelical scholar.

Karris, Robert J. "The Letter to the Galatians." In *New Collegeville Bible Commentary: New Testament*, edited by Daniel Durken, 581–601. Collegeville, MN: Liturgical Press, 2009. A modest and popular interpretation of the letter from a Catholic perspective.

Williams, Sam K. *Galatians*. ANTC. Nashville: Abingdon, 1997. Part of a series of commentaries intended to help pastors.

Witherup, Ronald D. "Galatians." In *The Paulist Biblical Commentary*, edited by Enrique Aguilar Chiu, et al., 1380–99. Mahwah, NJ: Paulist Press, 2018. A short, popular version of this commentary.

Wright, Tom (N. T.). *Paul for Everyone: Galatians and Thessalonians*. NTE. Louisville, KY: Westminster John Knox, 2004, 1–86. A brief and lively interpretation of Galatians from one of the most widely respected contemporary experts on Paul.

FOREIGN LANGUAGE COMMENTARIES

Bonnard, Pierre. *L'Épitre de Saint Paul aux Galates*. 2nd ed. Neuchâtel: Delachaux et Niestlé, 1972.

Cothenet, Edouard. *L'épitre aux Galates*. CaE 34. Paris: Éditions du Cerf, 1980.

Donegani, Isabel, et al. *La lettre aux Galates. "C'est pour la liberté que le Christ nous a libérés."* Les Cahiers de l'ABC 3. Saint-Maurice (Switzerland), 2015. Part of a series of "ABC" books to assist French speakers to work their way through the complexities of Galatians.

Lagrange, Marie-Joseph. *Saint Paul, Épitre aux Galates*. Paris: Gabalda, 1948; orig. 1918.

Légasse, Simon. *L'Épître de Paul aux Galates*. LD 9. Paris: Éditions du Cerf, 2000.

Lémonon, Jean-Pierre. *L'Épître aux Galates*. CBNT 9. Paris: Éditions du Cerf, 2008. The author's more technical commentary.

———. *Pour lire l'Épître aux Galates*. Paris: Éditions du Cerf/Mediaspaul, 2012. Part of a series of popular commentaries for French speakers, this is a practical "workbook"-style commentary, with helpful explanatory charts and suggestions for working through passages on one's own.

Vanhoye, Albert. *Lettera ai Galatai*. Milan: Paoline, 2000. The original Italian version of the commentary listed above in the CCSS series, but with its more technical observations intact.

OTHER BOOKS

Barrett, C. K. *Freedom and Obligation: A Study of the Epistle to the Galatians*. Philadelphia: Westminster, 1985.

deSilva, David A. *Galatians: A Handbook on the Greek Text*. Waco, TX: Baylor University Press, 2014. An indispensable tool for understanding the Greek text.

Dunn, James D. G. *The Theology of Paul's Letter to the Galatians*. Cambridge: Cambridge University Press, 1993. A very insightful summary of Paul's theological perspective in Galatians.

Gorman, Michael J. *Apostle of the Crucified Lord. A Theological Introduction to Paul and His Letters*. 2nd ed. Grand Rapids: Eerdmans, 2017, 227–72. Part of a general textbook introducing Paul and his thought, this is an expert summary of the letter, with an emphasis on the power of the cross and what the author terms "cruciformity," life lived configured to the cross of Christ.

Martini, Carlo Maria. *The Testimony of St. Paul: Meditations on the Life and Letters of St. Paul*. Translated by Susan Leslie. Middlegreen, Slough, UK: St. Paul, 1983. A pastorally sensitive reflection on Paul's teachings in general, with comments on Galatians.

McClendon, P. Adam. *Paul's Spirituality in Galatians: A Critique of Contemporary Christian Spiritualities*. Eugene, OR: Wipf & Stock, 2015. An interesting study in Paul's spirituality that offers an extensive analysis of Galatians 2:20.

Murphy-O'Connor, Jerome. *Keys to Galatians: Collected Essays*. Collegeville, MN: Liturgical Press, 2012. A collection of scholarly essays by a very creative interpreter of Paul.

Nanos, Mark D. *The Irony in Galatians: Paul's Letter in First-Century Context*. Minneapolis: Augsburg Fortress, 2002. A technical and highly creative analysis of Galatians in its historical context and from a Jewish perspective.

Owens, Mark D. *As It Was in the Beginning: An Intertextual Analysis of New Creation in Galatians, 2 Corinthians, and Ephesians*. Eugene, OR: Pickwick, 2015. A dissertation that offers a thorough study of the new creation theme in Judaism and in Paul and shows interconnectedness between the three letters in the subtitle.

INDEX OF NAMES

INDEX OF TOPICS

Nabatea, 32–33
New creation, 7, 113–14

Opponents of Paul, 9–10, 24, 95

Peace, 17–18, 114
Pedagogue, 73, 78
Pneumatology, 64
Promise, 70

Rabbinic interpretation, 5, 72
Redemption, 69, 80
Resurrection, 16
Revelation, 30
Rhetoric, 5, 10
Right hand/left hand, 47–48

Salvation, 19, 78, 90
Scribe (amanuensis), 16, 111

Scripture, 9, 68, 69
Sin(s), 18, 19
Slavery, 26, 77, 88, 98
Son, 80
Spirit (Holy Spirit), 63–64
Stigmata, 111–12

Testament, 71
Torah, 53
Trinity, 18, 80

Vatican Council II, 87

Will. *See* Testament
Works of the law, 53–54, 94, 101

Yeast. *See* Leaven

ILLUSTRATION CREDITS

The following illustrations are courtesy of Wikimedia Commons: Map of Asia Minor in the early first century CE, photograph by Jerry Caliunic; Ancient manuscript of Galatians (ca. 200 CE), photograph from University of Michigan; Ancient Greek slave working in a mine (ca. 490 BCE), photograph by Christophe Nave; *The Conversion of St. Paul* by Caravaggio (ca. 1600 CE), photograph by Jarek Tuszyński; *Moses Receiving the Tablets of Law* by Marc Chagall (ca. 1966 CE), photograph by Rokos Cornelis; An open torah scroll, photograph by Lawrie Cate; *Crucifixion* by Bernardino Luini (ca. 1530 CE), photograph by Trzęsacz; Roman collared slaves, photograph by Jun; *Abraham Dismissing Hagar and Ishmael* by Nicolaes Maes (1653 CE), photograph by Jane Darnell; *St. Francis of Assisi Receiving the Stigmata* by Peter Paul Rubens (ca. 1650 CE), photograph by Jarek Tuszyński.

Map of ancient Nabataea (1770 CE), adapted from Map of Judea, Samaria, and Surrounding Areas in New Testament Times created by Robert Cronan of Lucidity Design, LLC., published in *The Paulist Biblical Commentary* (Mahwah, NJ: Paulist Press, 2018).

Two Greco-Roman athletes wrestling, photograph of stone tablet relief at Musée du Louvre, Paris, France, photographer unknown.

Icon of the apostles Sts. Peter and Paul, photograph by Dmitry Kalinovsky/Dreamstime.com.

The Three Angels Visiting Abraham, from the Story of Abraham by Georg Pencz (ca. 1500–1550 CE), photograph by agefotostock/Alamy Stock Photo.

Madaba map of Jerusalem, located at St. George's Church, Madaba (biblical Medeba), Jordan, photograph by WitR/Shutterstock, Inc.

Map of first-century Jerusalem by Frank Sabatte, CSP, adapted from chapter 6 of Pheme Perkins, *Reading the New Testament: An Introduction*, 3rd ed. (Mahwah, NJ: Paulist Press, 2012).